The *DOCTRINE* of GOD

*A thesis submitted in fulfillment of
the requirements for the degrees of
Master's in Theology and Doctorate in Theology*

Rev. Dr. Ethel L. Williams

Christian Bible Center and Institute
2002

ISBN 979-8-88832-123-2 (paperback)
ISBN 979-8-88832-124-9 (digital)

Christian Faith Publishing
832 Park Avenue
Meadville, PA 16335
www.christianfaithpublishing.com

Printed in the United States of America

In memory of my grandmother Rev. Dr. Ethel Lee Williams. She was a God-fearing and devoted Christian. I admire the faith in God that she expressed in her daily life. She touched the young and old doing God's work. She showed many the path to a righteous and just life. It is for these reasons I have published her work. My hope is that by sharing her work, it will be an inspiration to people in the world seeking truth to life.

CONTENTS

Acknowledgments

First, I wish to express my gratitude to God. I also would like to thank the late Dr. Edward H. Boyce, author of *Between Now and Eternity*; Dr. Shammah Womack, author of *The Doctrine and Science of God*; Dr. William Evans, author of *The Great Doctrine of the Bible*.

My nephew, Neal C. Murray; grandson, LeRoy Simmons Jr. and granddaughter, Yolanda Simmons; and Judy McClain for their time and help with the printing of this thesis.

The doctrine herein is dealt with from the biblical standpoint rather than dogmatic theology. This is evident from the plan which followed in work, namely: together, all Scripture passages dealing with the subject under consideration and from those that may be called representatives; then seek to understand the meanings of these references by the study of the text itself as well as its context and parallel passages; and finally, from the selected proof—texts formulate the doctrinal teaching—and place such results under appropriate headings.

Theology is the greatest of all sciences, and anyone who has not had a comprehensive view of the subject is not qualified to deal with the sin question. Theology notes God's character and distinguishes his actions between the sinner and the saint.

The seven foremost doctrines of the Christian Church are the doctrine of God, the doctrine of Christ, the doctrine of the Holy Spirit, the doctrine of Satan, the doctrine of man, the doctrine of sin, and the doctrine of salvation.

Theology denotes the names and titles of God by which he is known. This is especially true of the doctrine of God. Theology is that branch of biblical science which treats the existence, nature and attributes of God, his relationship to man and the universe, and man's relationship and obligation to God.

I realize that it is not humanly possible to deal with every element of this vast subject in a thesis of this kind. However, I shall endeavor to deal with it briefly to the best of my knowledge and ability. My sole purpose in writing this thesis is to unfold the undeniable fact that the Old and New Testaments, which consist of not just words, but living words, contain life for whosoever will accept them.

Thus saith the Lord, Let not the wise man glory in
his wisdom, neither let the mighty man glory in his
might, let not the rich man glory in his riches:
But let him that glorieth glory in this, that he understandeth
and knoweth me, that I am the Lord which exercise
lovingkindness, judgment, and righteousness, in the
earth: for in these things I delight, saith the Lord.

—Jeremiah 9:23–24 KJV

CHAPTER 1

The Doctrine of God

The Existence of God

Taken for Granted by the Scripture Writers

It does not seem to have occurred to any of the writers of either the Old Testament or New Testament to attempt to prove or to argue the existence of God. Everywhere and at times, it is a fact that is taken for granted. A God capable of proof would be no God at all. He is the Self-Existent One (Exodus 3:14) and the source of all life. For as the Father hath life in himself: so hath he given to the Son to have life in himself ((John 5:26).

The sublime opening of the scriptures announces the fact of God and his existence, *"In the beginning God"* (Genesis 1:1). The rise or dawn of the idea of God in the mind of man is not depicted. Psalm 14:1 declares, *"the fool hath said in his heart, there is no God."* This does not indicate disbelief in the existence, but rather in the active interest of God in the affairs of men. He seemed to hide himself from the affairs of men (Job 22:12–14). The scriptures further recognize that men not only know the existence of God but have also a certain circle of ideas as to who and what he is (Romans 1:18–19). W. Evans states:

> No one but a "fool" will deny the fact of God. What! No God? A watch, and no key for it? A watch with a main-spring broken, and no jeweler to fix it? A lamp lit, and nobody to pour oil in to keep the wick burning? A garden, and no gardener? Flowers, and no florist? Conditions, and no conditioner? He that sitteth in heaven shall laugh at such absurd atheism.[1]

---

[1] W. Evans, *The Great Doctrines of the Bible*, 13.

Arguments for the Existence of God

These arguments may not prove conclusively that God is, but they do show that in order to explain the existence of any knowledge, thought, reason, conscience in man, *"we must assume that God is."* It is said of the beautiful, *"It may be shown, but not proved."* Likewise, we can also say of the existence of God. These arguments are probable, not demonstrative. For this reason, they supplement each other and constitute a series of evidence, which are cumulative in their nature. Though taken singly, none of them can be considered absolutely decisive; together, they furnish a corroboration of our primitive conviction of God's existence, which is of great practical value and is in itself insufficient to bind the moral actions of men.

A bundle of rods may not be broken even though each one separately may; the strength of the bundle is the strength of the whole. If in practical affairs we were to hesitate to act until we have absolute and demonstrable certainty, we would never begin to move all. Instead of doubting everything that can be doubted, let us rather doubt nothing until we are compelled to doubt. The late Dr. Orr said:

> What we mean by the proof of God's existence is simply that there are necessary acts of thought by which we rise from the finite to infinite, from the caused to the uncaused, from the contingent to the necessary from the reason involved in the structure of the universe to a universe and eternal reason, which is the ground of all, from morality in conscience to a moral Lawgiver and judge.
>
> In this connection the theoretical Proofs constitute an inseparable Unity—"constitute together," as Dr. Sterling declares, but the undulations of a single wave, which wave is but a natural rise and accent to God, on the part of man's own thought, with man's own experiences and consciousness as the object before him. Religion

was not produced by proofs of God's existence, and will not be destroyed by its sufficiency to some minds. Religion existed before argument; in fact, it is the preciousness of religion that leads to the seeking for all possible confirmations of the reality of God.[2]

---

[2] W. Evans, *The Great Doctrines of the Bible*, 14.

Universality of Belief: The Fact Stated and Proven

Man everywhere believes in the existence of a Supreme Being or beings to whom he is morally responsible and to whom propitiation needs to be made. Such belief may be crudely, even grotesquely, stated and manifested, but the validity of the fact is no more invalidated by such crudeness than the existence of a father is invalidated by the crude attempts of a child to draw a picture of his father.

It has been claimed by some that there are or were tribes in inland Africa that possessed no idea or conception of God. Moffat, Livingstone's father-in-law, made such a claim, but Livingstone, after a thorough study of the customs and languages of such tribes, conclusively showed that Moffat was wrong. The existence of such few tribes, even if granted, should not violate the fact we are here considering. Any more than the existence of some few men who are blind, lame, deaf, and dumb would make untrue the statement, and the fact that man is a seeing, hearing, speaking, and walking creature. The fact that some nations do not have a multiplication table does no violence to arithmetic.

Concerning so-called atheists in Christian lands, Hume, known as a famous skeptic, is reported to have said to Ferguson, as together they looked up into the starry sky: "Adam, there is a God." Voltaire, the atheist, prayed to God in a thunderstorm. Ingersoll, when charged with being an atheist, indignantly refuted the charge, saying: "I am not an atheist; I do not say that there is no God." "I thank God that I am an atheist," were the opening words of an argument to disprove the existence of God. A new convert of atheism was once heard to say to a coterie of unbelievers: "I have gotten rid of the idea of a supreme Being, and I thank God for it."

This universal belief does not come from outside sources, such as reason, tradition, or even the scripture, nor from reason or argument. Many could not intellectually believe in God by arguing and reasoning. Others who have great power of intellect and who have reasoned and argued on the subject are professed disbelievers in God.

This belief in God is not the result of logical arguments, or the Bible would have given us proof. Nor did this universal belief come from tradition for "tradition," says Dr. Patton, "can perpetuate only what has been originated. Nor can it be said that this belief came from the scripture? Even though it has been well said, unless man had knowledge of God from whom the Scriptures came, the revelation itself could have no authority for him. The very idea of scripture as revelation presupposes in a God who can make it." Dr. Neuman Smith continues, "Revelation must assume the existence of God."

This universal belief comes from within man. All of the evidence points to the conclusive facts that this universal faith in the existence of God is innate in man. It is inborn, natural, native, inherent, congenital-existing at the time of birth of someone born with innate kindness and comes from natural intuition. The power to know without reasoning, the feeling of understanding that something will happen or happens. Which results are, an example of this, a piece of knowledge that results in intuition.

Universality of Belief: From Whence Comes This Universal Belief?

This universal belief does not come from outside sources such as reason, tradition, or even the Scriptures. This universal belief in the existence of God does not come from reason of argument for many who believe in God have not given any time to reasoning and arguing the question. Some, indeed, intellectually, could not. Others who have great powers of intellect and who have reasoned and argued on the subject are professed disbelievers in God. Belief in God is not the result of logical arguments, or else the Bible would have given us proof.

The fact that all men everywhere believe in the existence of a Supreme Being or beings to whom they are morally responsible is a strong argument in favor of the truth. An effect must have a cause as universal; otherwise, we have an effect without an assignable cause. Certain it is that this argument makes the burden of proof to rest upon those who deny the existence of God.

The Argument from Cause: Cosmological

When we see a thing, we naturally ask for the cause of that thing. We see this world in which we live and ask how it came to be. It is self-originating, or is the cause of it being outside of itself? Is its cause finite or infinite? That it could not come into being of itself seems obvious; no more than nails, brick, mortar, wood, paint, color, or form into a house or building of themselves; no more than the type composing a book came into order of itself. When Liebig was asked if he believed that the grass and flowers which he saw around him grew by mere chemical forces, he replied, "No, no more than I could believe that the books on Botany describing them could grow more chemical forces."

No theory of an *eternal series* can account for this created universe. No matter how long a chain you may have, you must have a staple from where it depends. An endless perpendicular chain is an impossibility. "Every house is built by some man," says the Bible Hebrews 3:4. So this world in which we live was built by a designing mind of infinite power and wisdom. So it is when we consider man—man exists, but he owes his existence to some cause. Is this cause within or without himself? Finite or infinite? Trace our origin back, if you will, to our first parent, Adam. Then you must ask, "How did he come into being?" The doctrine of the eternity of man cannot be supported. Man is an effect he has not always existed, and geology proves this. That the first cause must have been an intelligent being is proven by the fact that we are intelligent beings ourselves.

The Argument from Design: Teleological

A watch proves only a maker, an artifact, but also a designer. A watch is made for a purpose; this is evident in its structure. A thoughtful, designing mind was the origin of the watch. So it is with the world in which we live. The "ends" in nature are not to be attributed to "natural results"—results which are produced without intelligence nor are they "the survival of the fittest," instances in which "accident and fortuity have done the work of mind." No, they are the results of a superintending and originating intelligence and will.

The Argument from Being: Ontological

Man has an idea of an infinite and perfect Being. From whence is this idea? Is it from finite and imperfect beings like ourselves? Certainly not. Therefore, this idea argues for the existence of an infinite and perfect Being: such a Being must exist, as a person, and not a mere thought.

The Moral Argument: Anthropological

Man has an intellectual and moral nature; hence, his Creator must be an intellectual and moral Being, a Judge, and Lawgiver. Man has an emotional nature. Only a Being of goodness, power, love, wisdom, and holiness could satisfy such a nature. These things denote the existence of a personal God.

Conscience in man says: "Thou shalt" and "Thou shalt not," "I ought" and "I ought not." These mandates are not self-imposed. They imply the existence of a Moral Governor to whom we are responsible. Cardinal Newman says:

> Were it not for the voice speaking so clearly
> in my conscience and my heart, I should be an
> atheist, or a pantheist, when I looked into the

world. Some things are wrong, others right love
is right, hatred is wrong. A thing is not simply
right because it pleases, or wrong because it dis-
pleases. Where did we get this standard of right
and wrong? Morality is obligatory? Who has a
right to command any life? We must believe that
there is a God, or believe that the very root of our
nature is a lie.[3]

The Argument from Congruity

If we have a key which fits all wards of the lock, we know that it
is the right key. If we have a theory which fits all facts in the case, we
know then that we have the right theory. Patton states:

> Belief in a self-existent, personal God is in
> harmony with all the facts of our mental and
> moral nature, as well as with all the phenomena
> of the natural world.
>
> If God exists, a universal belief in His exis-
> tence is natural enough; the irresistible impulse
> to ask for a first cause is accounted for; our reli-
> gious nature has an object; the uniformity of nat-
> ural law finds adequate explanation, and human
> history is vindicated from the charge of being a
> vast imposture.
>
> Atheism leaves all these matters without
> an explanation, and makes, not history alone,
> but our moral and intellectual nature itself, an
> imposture, and a lie.[4]

---

[3] W. Evans, *The Great Doctrines of the Bible*, 17.

[4] W. Evans, *The Great Doctrines of the Bible*, 18.

Scripture Arguments for Existence

A great deal of our knowledge rests upon the testimony of others. Now, the Bible is competent testimony. It is enough to satisfy us to the habits, customs, and manners of the people of the countries they visit, and which we have never seen; why is not the Bible, if it is authentic history, enough to satisfy us with its evidence as to the existence of God (Psalm 14:1, Job 22:12–14, Romans 1:18–19)?

Some facts need more evidence than others, we know. This is true of the fact of the existence of God. But the Bible history is sufficient to satisfy every reasonable demand. The history of the Jews and their prophecies are not explainable minus God. If we cannot believe in the existence of God on the testimony of the Bible, we might as well burn our books of history. A man cannot deny the truth of the testimony of the Bible unless he says plainly, *"No amount of testimony will convince me of the supernatural."*

Scripture does not attempt to prove the existence of God. It asserts, assumes, and declares that the knowledge of God is universal (Romans 1:19–21, 28, 32 and Romans 2:15). It asserts that God has wrought this great truth in the very warp and woof of every man's being so that nowhere is he without this witness. W. Evans states:

> The preacher may, therefore, safely follow
> the example of Scripture in assuming that there
> is a God. Indeed, he must unhesitatingly and
> explicitly assert it as the Scripture does, believing

that "His eternal power and divinity" are things that are clearly seen and perceived through evidences of His handiwork which abound on every hand.[5]

---

[5] W. Evans, *The Great Doctrines of the Bible*, 18.

CHAPTER 2

The Nature, Decrees, and Works of God

THE NATURE

The Spirituality of God vs. Materialism "God is Spirit"

To clarify the meaning concerning the statement of the fact "God is Spirit" (John 4:24): The Samaritan woman's question, "Where is God to be found? On Mt. Zion or Gerizim?"

Christ answers, "God is not be confined to any one place" (cf. Acts 48, Acts 17, 25, 1 Kings 8:27). God must be worshipped in spirit as distinguished from place, form, or other sensual limitations (John 4:21) and in truth, as distinguished from false conceptions resulting from imperfect knowledge (John 4:22).

Additional light on "God is Spirit" from other scriptures: according to Luke 24:39, "A spirit hath not flesh and bones," which means that it does not have a body or parts like human beings; it is incorporeal and is not subject to human limitations. Colossians 1:15 states, "The image of the invisible God." In 1 Timothy 1:17, it again reassures, "Now unto the King incorruptible, invisible." These passages teach that God has nothing of a material or bodily nature. Sight sees only objects of the material world, but God is not of the nature of the material world. Hence, he cannot be seen with the material eye—at least, not now.

A definition of "God is Spirit": God is invisible, incorporeal, without parts, without body, without passion, and therefore free from all limitations. He is apprehended not by the senses, but by the soul; hence, God is above sensuous perceptions. One Corinthians 2:6–16 intimates that without the teaching of God's spirit, we cannot know God. W. Evans states:

> "La place swept the heavens with his telescope, but he could not find anywhere a God. He

might just as well have swept a kitchen with his broom." Since God is not a material Being, He cannot be apprehended by physical means.[6]

There are questions and problems with the statement that, "God is Spirit." What is meant by that statement that man was made in the in image of God? Colossians 3:10 and Ephesians 2:24 declare that this "image" consists in "righteousness, knowledge, and holiness of truth." By that, I mean the image of God in man consists in intellectual and moral likeness, rather than physical resemblance. Some people think that I Thessalonians 5:23 suggests that the "Trinity of man"—body, soul, and spirit constitutes that image and likeness.

What is meant by the anthropomorphic expressions used by God? W. Evans states:

> For example, God is said to have hands, feet, arms, eyes, ears; He sees, feels, hears, walks, etc. Such expressions are to be understood only in the sense of human expressions being used in order to bring the infinite within the comprehension of the finite. How, otherwise, could we understand the concept of God saving by means of human expressions, in figures that we all can understand![7]

Spirit can be manifested in visible forms. It is written in John 1:32; "I saw the spirit descending from heaven like a dove" (or in the form of a dove). So throughout the ages, the invisible God has manifested Himself in visible form. This also occurred in Judges 6:34, "The Spirit of the Lord clothed Himself with Gideon."

On this truth is based the doctrine of "The Angels of the Lord" in the Old Testament. Genesis 16:7, 10, 13, note how the angel of

---

6   W. Evans, *The Great Doctrines of the Bible*, 19.
7   W. Evans, *The Great Doctrines of the Bible*, 20.

the Lord is identified with Jehovah himself (cf. v. 10, 13). In addition, Genesis 22:11–12 says, "And the angel of the LORD called unto him out of heaven, and said, Abraham, Abraham: and he said, Here I am. And he said, Lay not thine hand upon the lad, neither do thou anything unto him;…thou has not withheld thy son, thine only son from me."

In Genesis 18:1–16, one of the three angels clearly and definitely identifies himself with Jehovah. Compare chapter 19, where it is seen that only two angels have come to Sodom; the other has remained behind. Who was this one remaining angel? Genesis 18:17, 20 answers the question. Verse 22 reads, "And Abraham stood yet before the Lord." In Exodus 13:21, it is Jehovah while in 14:19, it is the angel that went before Israel. Thus was the way prepared for the incarnation for the Angel of the Lord in the Old Testament is undoubtedly the second person of the Trinity. This seems evident from Judges 13:18 and Isaiah 9:6, where both passages clearly refer to Christ and the name "Wonderful" occurs. Also, the omission of the definite article "the" from before the expression, "Angel of the Lord," and the substitution of "an" points the same truth. This change is made in the *revised version*.

What was it then that the elders of Israel saw when it is said they saw the God of Israel? Certainly, it was not God in his real essence for no man can have that vision and live. In John 1:18, the emphasis is on the word "God" and may read "no man hath seen God at any time." In John 5:37, Jesus says, "Ye have neither heard his voice at any time, nor seen his shape." W. Evans states:

> From this it seems clear that the 'seeing' here, to which has been the privilege of no man, refers to the essence rather than to the person of God, if such a distinction can really be made.[8]

None but the Son has really seen God as he really is. What then did these men see?

---

[8] W. Evans, *The Great Doctrines of the Bible*, 20–21.

Evidently, an appearance of God in some form to their outward senses; perhaps the form of a man since mention is made of his "feet." The vision may have been too bright for human eyes to gaze upon fully, but it was a vision of God. Yet it was only a manifestation of God for, although in Exodus 33:28, Moses was conversing with God, he yet said, "If I have found grace in thy sight, show me thy face." Moses had been granted exceeding great and precious privileges in that he had been admitted into close communion with God, more so than any other member of the human race. But, still dissatisfied, he longed for more. Therefore, in verse 18, he asks to see the unveiled glory of God—that very thing which no man in the flesh can ever see and live.

By reading Exodus 33:18–23, we find God's answer: "Thou canst not see my face… Thou shalt see my back parts, but my face shalt not be seen." Numbers 12:8 throws light upon the subject, if compared with Exodus 33:11. W. Evans states:

> The secret remained unseen, the longing unsatisfied, and the nearest approach to the good vision reached him, with whom God spake face to face, as friend with friend, was to be hidden in the cleft of the rock, to be made aware of an awful shadow, and to hear the voice of the unseen.[9]

---

[9] W. Evans, *The Great Doctrines of the Bible*, 21–22.

The Decrees

It is important to note Webster Dictionary's definition of the word *decrees*.

> A *decree* is an authoritative order or decision
> deciding what is, or is to be done; edit. A collec-
> tion of Church laws; as the Decree of Gratain.
> Lastly, an eternal purpose of God for ordaining
> some event or condition.[10]

---

10 *New Compact Webster Dictionary*, 446–447.

The Work of Jesus Christ

The birth of Jesus Christ is important and has a supreme place in the Christian religion. Christianity is distinctly a religion of atonement. The elimination of the doctrine of the death of Christ from the religion that bears his name would mean the surrender of its uniqueness and claim to be the only true religion. It is its redemptive feature that distinguishes Christianity from all other religions. If you surrender this distinctive Christian doctrine from its creed, then this supreme religion is brought down to the level of many other prevailing religious systems. Christianity is not merely a system of ethics. It is the history of redemption through Jesus Christ, the personal Redeemer.

The atonement has a vital relation to Jesus Christ. The atonement is so closely related to Jesus Christ, to his work, as set forth in the Scriptures, that it is absolutely inseparable from it. Christ was not primarily a religious teacher, a philanthropist, or an ethical example. He was all these and so much more. He was, first and foremost, the world's Savior and Redeemer. Other great men have been valued for their lives. He, above all, for his death, in which God and man are reconciled.

The cross is the magnet which sends the electric current through the telegraph between earth and heaven. It makes both the Old and New Testaments trill through the ages of the past and future, with living, harmonious, and saving truth. Let us understand that the power of Christianity lies not in hazy indefiniteness, not in shadowy forms, not so much even in definite truths and doctrines, but in the truth and in the doctrine of Christ crucified and risen from the dead. Unless Christianity be more than ethical, it is not, nor can it really be, ethical at all. It is redemptive, dynamic through that redemption, and ethical withal. W. Evans states:

> Paul says, "I deliver unto you first of all, first in order: the first plank in the gospel platform; the truth of primary importance—that Christ died for our sins" (1 Corinthians 15:1–3). There can be no gospel story message or preaching without the story of the death of Christ as the Redeemer of men.[11]

---

[11] W. Evans, *The Great Doctrines of the Bible*, 70–71.

Definition of Personality

Personality exists where there is intelligence, mind, will, reason, individuality, self-consciousness, and self-determination. There must not be mere consciousness only for the beast has that, but self-consciousness. Nor is personality determination for the beast has this too. Even though this determination is the result of influences from without, self-determination, the power by which men acts of his own freewill determines his acts from within. Neither corporeity nor substance (as we understand these words) are necessarily, if at all, involved in personality. There may be true personality without either or both of these.

When it comes to Scripture teaching on the personality of God, it would be well to refer to the ontological argument for the existence of God in Exodus 3:14:1 "I Am That I Am." This name is wonderfully significant. Its central idea is that of existence and personality. The words signify "I Am, I Was, I Shall Be" and are suggestively corresponding with the New Testament concerning God "Which is, and which was, and which is to come" (Revelation 1:4).

All the names given to God in the Scripture denote personality. Here are some of them: Jehovah Jireh—the Lord will provide (Genesis 22:13, 14); Jehovah-Rapha—the Lord that healeth (Exodus 15:26); Jehovah Nissi—the Lord our Banner (Exodus 17:8–15); Jehovah Shalom—the Lord our Peace (Judges 6:24); Jehovah Raah—the Lord is my Shepherd (Psalm 23:1); Jehovah Tsidkenu—the Lord our Righteousness (Jeremiah 23:6); and Jehovah Sahmmah—the Lord is Present (Ezekiel 48:35). Moreover, the personal pronouns ascribed to God prove personality. For example: "That they might know thee, the only true God and Jesus Christ whom thou hath sent" (John 17:3).

All through the Scriptures, there are names and personal pronouns ascribed to God, which undeniably prove that God is a person. A sharp distinction is drawn in the Scriptures between the Gods of the heavens and the Lord God of Israel. See Jeremiah 10:1–10 states:

> Note the context in verses 3–9; idols are things, not persons; they cannot walk, speak, do good or evil. God is wiser than the men who made these idols. If the idol makers are persons, much more is God. When reading Acts 14:15; 1 Thessalonians 1:9; and Psalm 94:9–10, one can see the sharp contrast drawn between dead idols and the living, personal, true and only God. For God is to be clearly distinguished from things which have no life, He is a living person.[12]

It is clear that the attributes of personality are ascribed to God in scripture. In Genesis 6:6, God repents; in Genesis 6:6, he grieves; in 1 King 11:9, he's angry; in Deuteronomy 6:15, he is jealous; in Revelation 3:19, he loves; and in Proverbs 6:16, he hates.

God possesses the attributes of personality and, therefore, is a person. The relation which God bears to the universe and to men, as set forth in the scripture, can be explained on the basis that God is a person. W. Evans states:

> Deism maintains that God, while the Creator of the world, yet sustains no further relations to it. He made just as the clockmaker makes a self-winding clock. He makes it and then leaves it to run itself without any interference on his part. Such teaching as this finds no sanction in the Bible. What are God's relations to the universe and to man?[13]

---

[12] W. Evans, *The Great Doctrines of the Bible*, 22–23.

[13] W. Evans, *The Great Doctrines of the Bible*, 23–24.

He is the Creator of the universe and man. Genesis 1:1 and John 1:13 contain vital truths. The universe did not exist from eternity nor was it made from existing matter. It was not processed an emanation from the infinite but was summoned into being by the decree of God.

With this connection, the arguments from cause and design may be properly considered as W. Evans states:

> The creation of the universe and man prove the personality of the Creator—God. God sustains certain relations to the universe and man which he has made.[14]

Hebrews 1:31 states, "Who upholds all things." Colossians 1:15–17 says, "By Him all things hold together." Psalm 104:27–30 says, "All creatures wait upon Him for their meat in due season." Psalm 75:6–7 states, "Promotion cometh neither from the east, nor from the west, nor from the south. But God is judge: he putteth down one, and setteth up another.

> First, we learn that all things are held together by Him; if not, this old world would go to pieces quickly. The uniformity and accuracy of a natural law compels us to believe in a God who intelligently guides us to believe in a personal God who intelligently guides and governs the universe. Disbelief in this fact would mean utter confusion. It is not blind chance, but a personal God that is at the helm. Second, that the physical supplies for all God's creatures are in His hand. He feeds them all. What God gives we gather. If He withholds provisions we die. Third, that God has His hand in history, guiding and shaping the affairs of nations. Victor Hugo said, "Waterloo was God."

---

14 W. Evans, *The Great Doctrines of God*, 24.

Fourth, Consider with what detail God's care is described: The sparrows, the lilies, the hairs of the head, the tears of His children, etc.[15]

We can see how these facts are clearly portrayed in the following scriptures: Matthew 6:28–30, Matthew 10:29–30, Genesis 39:21, Genesis 50:20, Daniel 1:9, and Job 1:12.

The personality of God is shown by his active interest and participation in all things, even the smallest things, in the universe, the experience of man, and in the life of all his creatures.

The Personality vs. Pantheism

Pantheism maintains that this universe, in its ever-changing conditions, is but the manifestation of the one ever-changing universal substance which is God. Thus, everything is God, and God is everything. God is all, all is God. Thus, God is identified with nature and not held to be independent of and separate from it. God is, therefore, a necessary but a conscious force working in the world. W. Evans states:

> The bearing of the personality of God on idea of religion. True religion may be defined as the communion between two persons, God and man. Religion is a personal relationship between God in heaven and man on earth. If God were not a person there could be no communion; if both God and man were one there could be no communion, and consequently no religion. An independent personal relationship on both sides is absolutely necessary to communion. Man can have no communion with influence, a force, or an impersonal something; nor can an influence

---

[15] W. Evans, *The Great Doctrines of the Bible*, 24–25.

have any moving or affection towards man. It is absolutely necessary to the true definition of religion that both God and man be persons. God is a person, not force or influence.[16]

------

16 W. Evans, *The Great Doctrines of the Bible*, 22.

The Attributes: Moral Attributes

The Attributes of God. It is necessary to clearly distinguish between the attributes and the nature of God. It is maintained by some that such a division ought to be made, that these qualities of God which we call attributes are, in reality, part of his nature and essence. Whether this be exactly so or not, my purpose in speaking of the attributes of God is for convenience in the study of the doctrine of God.

It has been customary to divide the attributes of God into two classes: the natural and the moral. The natural are omniscience, omnipotence, omnipresence, and eternity. The moral attributes are holiness, righteousness, faithfulness, mercy and loving-kindness, and love.

The Natural Attributes: The Omniscience of God. God is spirit and, as such, has knowledge. He is a perfect Spirit and, as such, has perfect knowledge. Omniscience means that God knows all things and is absolutely perfect in knowledge. There are various scriptures that set forth the fact of God's omniscience. "Canst thou by searching find out God? Canst thou find out the Almighty unto perfection?" (Job 11:7). Job's friends professed to have discovered the reason for his affliction; had they not found out the secrets of the divine wisdom unto perfection?

Isaiah 40:28 reads, "There is no searching of his understanding." Joseph's captive condition might have led him to lose trust and faith in God. But Joseph had not seen all God's plans—no man has (Job 37:16).

Psalm 147:5 states that "His understanding is infinite." Of his understanding is no number, no computation. He who can number and name and call the stars is able to call each of them by name out of their captivity. His knowledge is not to be measured by ours. One John 3:20 states:

> God knows all things. Our hearts may pass over certain things, and fail to see some things that should be confessed. God, however, sees all things.

Romans 11:33 declares:

> "How unsearchable are His judgments, and His ways past finding out." The mysterious purposes and decrees of God touching man and his salvation are beyond all human comprehension.[17]

His knowledge is absolutely comprehensive. Proverbs 15:3 states, "The eyes of the Lord are in very place, keeping watch upon the evil and the good." Otherwise, how could he reward and punish? Not one single thing occurring in any place escapes his knowledge. Proverbs 5:21 says, "For the ways of man are before the eyes of the lord, and he pondereth all his goings." We may have habits hidden from our fellow creatures, but not from God.

God has a perfect knowledge of all that is in nature. Psalm 147:4 states, "He telleth the number of the stars; he calleth them all by their names."

God has a perfect knowledge of all that transpires in human experience. Proverbs 5:21 says, "For the ways of man are before the eyes of the Lord, and he pondereth all his goings." All of man's doings are weighted by God. How this should affect his conduct! Psalm 139:2 says that "Thou knowest my downsitting and mine uprising, thou understandest my thought afar off." W. Evan states:

> Thou compassest my path and my lying down, and art acquainted with all my ways.

---

[17] W. Evans, *The Great Doctrines of the Bible*, 28–29.

Before our thoughts are fully developed, our unspoken sentences, the rising feeling in our hearts, our activity, our resting, all that we do from day to day is known and sifted by God. In verse 4, "There is not a word in my tongue, but thou O Lord, knowest it altogether."[18]

This not only includes thoughts and purposes, but also words spoken—idle, good, or bad. Exodus 3:7 states, "I have seen the affliction…heard the cry: know the sorrows of my people which are in Egypt."

The tears and grief which they dared not show to their taskmasters, God saw and noted. Did God know of their trouble in Egypt? It seemed to them as though he did not, but he did. Matthew 10:29–30 says, "But the very hairs of your head are all numbered." What minute knowledge is this! Exodus 3:19 shows God's intimate knowledge as to what a single individual will do: "And I am sure that the king of Egypt will not let you go, no, not by a mighty hand."

Isaiah 48:18 states, "O that thou hadst hearkened to my commandments! Then had thy peace have been as a river." In this, we see what would have been if only we had acted and decided differently. W. Evans states:

God has a perfect knowledge of all that transpires in human history. With what precision are national changes and destinies foretold and depicted in Daniel 2:8, Acts 15:18 tells that "Known unto God are all His works from the beginning of the world (ages)." In the context surrounding this verse are clearly set forth the religious changes that were to characterized the generation to come, the which have been so far literally, though not fully, fulfilled.[19]

---

18 W. Evans, *The Great Doctrines of the Bible*, 29–30.
19 W. Evans, *The Great Doctrines of the Bible*, 30.

God knows from all eternity to all eternity what will take place. The omniscience of God is adduced as the proof that he alone is God, especially as contrasted with gods (idols) of the heathen. Isaiah 48:58 states, "I have even from the beginning declared it unto thee; before it came to pass I showed it thee… I have showed thee new things from this time, even hidden things."

In Isaiah 46:9–10, it says, "I am God…declaring the end from the beginning, and from ancient times the things that are not yet done, saying, My counsel shall stand, and I will do all my pleasure." Here, God is announcing to his prophets things that are to occur in the future; things which would have been impossible for the human understanding to know or reach. There is no past, present, or future with God. Everything is one great living present. We are like a man standing by a river in a low place, who, consequently, can see only that part of the river that passes by him; but he who is aloof in the air may see the whole course of the river, how it rises, and how it runs. Thus, is it with God.

There are certain problems in connection with the doctrine of the omniscience of God; how the divine intelligence can comprehend so vast and multitudinous and exhaustless a number of things must forever surpass our comprehension. Romans 11:33 says, "O the depth of the riches both of the wisdom and knowledge of God! How unsearchable are his judgments, and his ways past finding out!" There is no searching of his understanding; it is beyond human computation. We must expect, therefore, to stand amazed in the presence of such matchless wisdom and find problems in connection therewith, which must, for the time at least, remain unsolved.

Again, we must not confound the foreknowledge of God with his foreordination. The two things are, in a sense, distinct. The fact that God foreknows a thing makes that thing certain but not necessary. His foreordination is based upon his foreknowledge. The fact that Pharaoh was responsible for the hardening process was foreknown and foretold by God. The actions of men are considered certain but not necessarily by reason of the divine foreknowledge.

The Natural Attributes: The Omnipotence of God. The Omnipotence of God is that attribute by which he can bring to pass everything by which he wills. God's power admits of no bounds or limitations. God's declaration of his intention is the pledge of the thing intended being carried out. "Hath he said, and shall he not do it!"

In general, concerning the scriptural declaration of the fact, Job 42:2 says, "I know that thou canst do everything (all things), and that no thought can be withholden from thee." The mighty review of all God's works as it passes before Job (context) brings forth this confession: "There is no resisting thy might, and there is no purpose thou canst not carry out." Genesis 18:14 says, "Is anything too hard for the Lord?" What had ceased to be possible by natural means comes to pass by supernatural means.

Concerning the scriptural declaration of the fact in the world of nature. W. Evans states:

> Genesis 1:1–3 states, "God created the heaven and earth. And God said, let there be light, and there was light." Thus, He spoke and it was done. He commanded and it stood fast. He does not need even to give His hand to the work; His word is sufficient.[20]

Psalm 107:25–29 lets us know that:

> For he commandeth, and raiseth the stormy wind, which lifteth up the waves thereof.
> They mount up to the heaven, they go down again to the depths: their soul is melted because of trouble.
> They reel to and fro, and stagger like a drunken man, and are at their wit's end.
> Then they cry unto the Lord in their trouble, and he bringeth them out of their distresses.
> He maketh the storm a calm, so that the waves thereof are still.

---

[20] W. Evans, *The Great Doctrines of the Bible*, 32.

God's slightest word, once uttered, is a standing law to which all nature must absolutely conform. Nahum 1:5–6 states:

> The mountains quake at him, and the hills melt, and the earth is burned at his presence, yea, the world, and all that dwell therein.
> Who can stand before his indignation? And who can abide in the fierceness of his anger? His fury is poured out like fire, and the rocks are thrown down by Him.

W. Evans states:

> This is God's comforting message to Israel. Everything in the sky, in sea, on earth is absolutely subject to His control.[21]

When discussing the experience of mankind, how wonderfully this is illustrated in the experience of Nebuchadnezzar (Daniel 4) and in the conversion of Saul (Acts 9) as well as in the case of Pharaoh (Exodus 4:11). James 4:12–15 states, "For that ye ought to say, if the Lord will, we shall live and do this or that." All human actions, whether present or future, are dependent upon the will and power of God. These things are in God's—not in man's—power. This rings true in the parable of the rich fool in Luke 12:16–21.

The heavenly inhabitants are subject to his will and world. Daniel 4:35 states, "He doeth according to his will in the army of heaven." Hebrew 1:19 states, "Are they (angels) not all ministering spirits, sent forth to minister for them who shall be heirs of salvation?" It has been said that angels are being created by the power of God for some specific act of service, and that after that act of service is rendered, they pass out of existence.

Even Satan is under the control of God. Satan has no power over any of God's children except as God permits him to have. This

---

[21] W. Evans, *The Great Doctrines of the Bible*, 32–33.

fact is clearly established in the case of Job (Job 1:12, 2:6) and Peter (Luke 22:31–32). In these scriptures, we are told that Satan had petitioned God that he might sift the self-righteous patriarch and the impulsive apostle. Finally, Satan is to be forever bound with a great chain (Revelation 20:2). God can set a bar to the malignity of Satan just as he can set a bar to the waves of the sea.

The Natural Attributes: The Omnipresence of God. The omnipresence of God means that God is present everywhere. This attribute is closely connected with the omniscience and omnipotence of God for if God is everywhere present, he is everywhere active and possesses full knowledge of all that transpires in every place. W. Evans states:

> This does not mean that God is everywhere present in a bodily sense, nor even in the same sense. For there is a sense in which He may be in heaven, His dwelling place, in which He cannot be said to be elsewhere. We must guard against the pantheistic idea which claims that God is everywhere, while maintaining the Scriptural doctrine that He is everywhere present in all things. Pantheism emphasizes the omnipresent activity of God, but denies His personality. Those holding the doctrine of pantheism make loud claims to philosophic ability and high intellectual training. But is it not remarkable that it is in connection with this very phase of the doctrine of God that the Apostle Paul says, "They became fools?" (Romans 1). God is everywhere and in every place; His center is everywhere; His circumference nowhere. But this presence is a spiritual and not a material presence, yet it is a real presence[22]

---

[22] W. Evans, *The Great Doctrines of the Bible*, 33–34.

In Jeremiah 23:23–24, it reads, "Am I a God at hand, saith the Lord, and not a God afar of? Can any hide himself in secret places that I shall not see him? Saith the Lord. Do not I fill heaven and earth? Saith the Lord." Did the false prophets think they could hide their secret crimes from God? Or that he could not pursue them into foreign countries? Or that he knew what was transpiring in heaven only and not upon the earth, and even in its most distant corners? It was wrong for them to thus delude themselves; their sins would be detected and punished (Psalm 10:1–14).

Psalm 139:7 asks, "Whither shall I go from thy spirit, or whither shall I flee from thy presence." How wondrously the attributes of God are grouped in this Psalm. In verses 1–6, the Psalmist speaks of the omniscience of God; God knows him through and through. In verses 13–19, it is the omnipotence of God which overwhelms the Psalmist. The omnipresence of God is forth in verses 7–12. The Psalmist realizes that he is never out of the sight of God any more than he is outside of the range of his knowledge and power. God is in heaven, "Hell is naked before Him," souls in the intermediate states are fully known to him (cf. Job 26:2 and Jonah 2:2), and the darkness is as the light to him.

Job asks a simple question in chapter 22 verses 12–14: "Is not God in the height of heaven?… Can he judge through the dark cloud? Thick clouds are a covering to him that he seeth not." All agreed that God displayed his presence in the heaven, but Job had inferred from this that God could not know and did not take notice of such actions of men as were hidden behind the intervening clouds. Not that Job was atheistic, no, but probably denied God the attribute of omnipresence and omniscience.

In Acts 17:24–28, we read that "For in Him we live, and move, and have our being." Without his upholding hand, we must perish; God is our nearest environment. From these and many other scriptures, we are clearly taught that God is everywhere present and acting; there is no place where God is not. W. Evans states:

> This does not mean that God is everywhere
> present in the same sense. For we are told that

He is in heaven, His dwelling place (1 Kings 8:30); that Christ is at His right hand in heaven (Ephesians 1:20); that God's throne is in heaven (Revelation 21:2, Isaiah 66:1). We may summarize the doctrine of the Trinity thus, God the Father is specially manifested in heaven; God the Son has been specially manifested on the earth; God the spirit is manifest everywhere. Just as the soul is present in every part of the body so God is present in every part of the world.

In explaining some practical inferences from this doctrine, first, 'of comfort.' The nearest of God to the believer. "Speak to Him then for He listens. And spirit with Spirit can meet; Closer is He than breathing, and nearer than hands or feet. God is never so far off, as even to be near; He is within. Our spirit is the home He holds most dear, To think of Him by our side is almost as untrue, as to remove His shrine beyond those of starry blue." (Faber)

The omnipresence is not only a detective truth it is protective also. After dwelling on this great and awful attribute in Psalm 139, the psalmist in verses 17–18 exclaims, "How precious are thy thought to me…when I awake, I am still with thee."

By this is meant that God stands by our side to help, and as One who loves and understands us (Matthew 28:20). Second, 'of warning,' "As in the Roman empire the whole world was one great prison to a malefactor, and in his flight to the most distant lands the emperor could track him, so under the government of God, no sinner can escape the eye of the judge." Thus the omnipresence of God is detective as well as protective.

"Thou God seest me," should serve as warning to keep us from sin.[23]

The Eternity and Immutability of God. The word *eternal* is used in two senses in the Bible. First, figuratively, as denoting existence which may have a beginning but will have no end (e.g., angels, the human soul). Second, denoting an existence which has neither beginning nor ending, like that of God. Time has past, present, and future—eternity does not. Eternity is infinite duration without any beginning, end or limit, and ever-abiding present. We can conceive of it only as duration indefinitely extended from the present moment in two directions: as to the past and as to the future.

One of the deaf and dumb pupils in the institution of Paris, desiring to express his idea of the eternity of the deity, replied: "It is duration, without beginning or end; existence, without bounds or dimension; present, without past or future. His eternity is youth, without infancy or old age; life, without birth or death; today, without yesterday or tomorrow." W. Evans states:

> By the immutability of God is meant that God's nature is absolutely unchangeable. It is not possible that He should possess one attribute at one time that He does not possess at another. Nor can there be any change in the Deity for better or for worse. God remains forever the same. He is without beginning and without end; the self-existent "I Am"; He remains forever the same, and unchangeable.[24]

Concerning the scriptural fact of the eternity of God, Habakkuk 1:12 asks, "Art thou not from everlasting, O Lord my God, mine Holy One?" The Chaldeans had threatened to annihilate Israel. The

---

[23] W. Evans, *The Great Doctrines of the Bible*, 34–35.
[24] W. Evans, *The Great Doctrines of the Bible*, 35–36.

prophet could not believe it to be possible for has not God eternal purposes for Israel? Is He not holy? How, then, can evil triumph?

Psalm 90:2 says, "Before the mountains were brought forth, or ever thou hadst formed the earth and world, even from everlasting to everlasting, thou are God." Short and transitory is the life of man; with God, it is otherwise. The perishable nature of man is here compared with the imperishable nature of God. Psalm 102:24–27 says:

> I said, O my God, take me not away in the midst of my days: thy years are throughout all generations.
>
> Of old thou hast laid the foundations of the earth: and the heavens are thy work of thy hands.
>
> They shall perish, but thou shalt endure; yea, all of them shall wax old like a garment; as a vesture shalt thou change them, and they shall be changed.
>
> But thou art the same, and thy years shall have no end.

Hence, we find where the psalmist contrasts the imperishable nature of God. Exodus 3:14 tells us, "And God said unto Moses, I AM THAT I AM." The past, present, and future lie in these words the name of Jehovah. Revelation 1:8 further declares, "I am Alpha and Omega, the beginning and the ending, saith the Lord, which is, and which was, and which is to come, the Almighty."

A scriptural statement of the immutability of God is declared in Malachi 3:6: "I am the Lord, I change not." Man's hope lies in that fact as the context here shows. Man had changed in his life and purpose toward God, and if God, like man, had changed, man would have been destroyed. This is simply supported in James 1:17, "The Father of lights, with whom is no variables, either shadow of turning." W. Evans states:

> There is no change in the sense of the degree of intensity of light such as is manifested in the

heavenly bodies. Such lights are constantly varying and changing; not so with God. There is no inherent, indwelling, possible change in God. In Samuel 15:29, we read, "And also the Strength of Israel will not lie nor repent." From these scriptures we assert that God, in His nature and character, is absolutely without change".[25]

Does God Repent? What, then, shall we say with regard to such scriptures as Jonah 3:10 and Genesis 6:6?

And God repented of the evil, that He said He would do unto them. (Jonah 3:10)

And it repented the Lord that He had made man on the earth, and it grieved Him at his heart. (Genesis 6:6)

In reply, we may say that God does not change but threatens that men may change. W. Evan states:

The repentant attitude in God does not involve any real change in character and purposes of God. He ever hates the sin and ever pities and loves the sinner; that is so both before and after the sinner's repentance. Divine repentance is therefore the same principle acting differently in altered circumstances. If the prospect of punishment answers the same purpose as that intended by the punishment itself, then there is no inconsistency in its remission, for punishment is not an end, it is only a means to goodness, to the reign of the law of righteousness.[26]

---

[25] W. Evans, *The Great Doctrines of the Bible*, 36.
[26] W. Evans, *The Great Doctrines of the Bible*, 36–37.

When God appears to be displeased with anything or orders it differently from what we expected, we say, after that manner of men, that he repents. God's attitude toward the Ninevites had not changed, but they had changed. For they had changed from sin unto righteousness, God's attitude toward them and his intended dealings with them as sinners must of necessity change. Of course, God's character had, in no wise, changed with respect to these people, although his dealings with men change as they change from ungodliness to godliness, and from disobedience unto obedience.

THE MORAL ATTRIBUTES

The Holiness of God

If there is any difference of importance in the attributes of God, of that which his holiness seems to occupy the first place. It is, to say the least, the one attribute which God would have his people remember him by more than any other. In the visions of himself which God granted men in the Scriptures, the thing that stood out most prominently was the divine holiness. This is clearly seen by referring to the visions of Moses, Job, and Isaiah. Some thirty times does the Prophet Isaiah speak of Jehovah as "The Holy One," thus indicating what feature of those beatific visions had most impressed him.

The holiness of God is the message of the entire Old Testament. To the prophets, God was the absolutely Holy One; the one with eyes too pure to behold evil; the One swift to punish iniquity. In taking a photograph, the part of the body which we desire most to see is not the hands or feet, but the face. So is it with our vision of God. He desires us to see not his hand and finger, denoting his power and skill, nor even his throne as indicating his majesty. W. Evans states:

> It is His Holiness by which He desires to be remembered as, that is the attribute which most glorifies Him. Let us bear this fact in mind as we study this attribute of the divine nature. It is just this vision of God that we need today when the tendency to deny the reality or the awfulness of sin prevails. Our view of the necessity of the atonement will depend very largely upon our view of the holiness of God. Light views of God

and His holiness will produce light views of sin
and the atonement.[27]

There are several scriptural passages that set forth the fact of
God's holiness. Isaiah 57:15 states, "Thus saith the high and lofty
one that inhabiteth eternity, whose name is Holy; I dwell in the high
and holy place." In Psalm 99:9, we are encouraged to "Exalt the Lord
our God, and worship at His holy hill: for the Lord our God is holy."
Habakkuk 1:13 says, "Thou art of purer eyes than to behold evil,
and canst not look on iniquity." One Peter 1:15–16 says, "But as he
which hath called you holy, so be ye holy in all manner of conversa-
tion. Because it is written, Be ye holy: for I am holy."

God's personal name is *Holy*. John 17:17 issues a plea: "Holy
Father, keep through thine own name those whom thou hast given
me." Christ here contemplates the Father as the Holy One—as the
source and agent of that which he desires for his disciples, namely,
holiness of heart and life, being kept from the evil of this world. Is
it not remarkable that this attribute of holiness is ascribed to each of
the three persons of the trinity? God the Father is the Holy One of
Israel (Isaiah 41:4); God the Son is the Holy One (Acts 3:14); God
the Spirit is called the Holy Spirit (Ephesians 4:30). W. Evans states:

> The scriptural meaning of holiness as
> applied to God is suggested in Job 34:10, "Be it
> far from God, that he should do wickedness; and
> from the Almighty that He should commit iniq-
> uity." An evil God, one that could commit evil
> would be a contradiction in terms, an impossible,
> inconceivable idea. Job seemed to doubt that the
> principle on which the universe was conducted
> was one of absolute equity. He must know that
> God is free from all evildoing. However hidden
> the meaning of His dealings, He is always just.
> God never did, and never will do wrong to any

---

²⁷ W. Evans, *The Great Doctrines of the Bible*, 37–38.

of His creatures; He will never punish wrongly. Men may often do; God never does.

Leviticus 11:43–45: "Ye shall not make yourselves abominable with any creeping thing that creepeth, neither shall ye make yourselves unclean with them, that ye should be defiled thereby. For I am the Lord your God; ye shall therefore sanctify yourselves, and ye shall be holy; for I am Holy: neither shall ye defile yourselves with any manner of creeping thing that creepeth upon the earth… Ye shall therefore be holy, for I am Holy.[28]

This means that God is absolutely clean, pure, and free from all defilement. Consider the construction of the tabernacle, with its holy and most holy place into which the high priest alone entered once a year, the Ten Commandments, with their moral categories, the laws of clean and unclean animals and things. All these speak to us in unmistakable terms as to what is meant by holiness as applied to God.

Two things, by the way of definition, may be inferred from these Scriptures; first, negatively, that God is entirely apart from all that is evil and from all that defiles both in himself and in relation to all his creatures. Second, and positively, by the holiness of God, we mean the consummate holiness, perfection, purity, and absolute sanctity of his nature. There is absolutely nothing unholy in him. So the Apostle John declares, "God is light, and in him is no darkness at all" (1 John 1:5).

In speaking about the manifestation of God's holiness, Proverbs 15:9 states, "The way of the wicked is an abomination unto the Lord." The thoughts of the wicked are an abomination unto the Lord." God hates sin and is its uncompromising foe. Sin is a vile and detestable thing to God. Isaiah 59:1–2 says:

Behold, the Lord's hand is not shortened, that it cannot save; neither his ear heavy, that it cannot hear. But your iniquities have separated

---

[28] W. Evans, *The Great Doctrines of the Bible*, 38.

> or caused separation between you and your God,
> and your sins have hid his face from you, that he
> will not hear.

Israel's sin had raised a wall of partition. The infinite distance between the sinner and God is because of sin. The sinner and God are at opposite sides of the moral universe. This is in answer to Israel's charge of God's inability to save them. From these two scriptures, it is clear that God's holiness manifests itself in the hatred of sin and the separation of the sinner from himself. Whereby, this awful distance is made near by the atonement of the blood of Jesus shed on the cross.

Saint John 3:16 tells us, "For God so loved the world, that He gave his only begotten Son." Here, God's holiness is seen in that he loves righteousness in the life of his children to such a degree that he gave his only Son to secure it. W. Evans states:

> The Cross shows how much God loves holiness. The cross stands for God's holiness before even His love. For Christ died not merely for our sins, but in order that He might provide us with that righteousness of life which God loves. He died that we might be forgiven; He died to make us good. Do we love holiness to the extent of sacrificing for it?[29]

In understanding the practical deductions form the doctrine of God's holiness, we must first approach God with "reverence and godly fear" (Hebrews 12:28). In the story of Moses' approach to the burning bush, the smiting of the men at Beth Shemesh, and the boundary set about Mt. Sinai, we are taught to feel our own unworthiness. There is too much hilarity in our approach unto God. Ecclesiastes 5:13 inculcates great care in our address to God.

Second, we shall have views of sin when we get right views of God's holiness. Isaiah, the holiest man in all Israel, was cast down at

---

[29] W. Evans, *The Great Doctrines of the Bible*, 39–40.

the sight of his own sin he had seen the vision of God's holiness. The same thing is true of Job 40:35; 42:45. We confess sin in such easy and familiar terms that it has almost lost its terror for us.

Third, that approach to a holy God must be through the merits of Christ and on the round of a righteousness which is Christ's and which naturally we do not possess. Herein lies the need of the atonement.

The Righteousness and Justice of God

In a certain sense, the attributes are but the manifestation of God's holiness. It is holiness as manifested in dealing with the sons of men. Holiness has to do more particularly with the character of God in itself while in righteousness and justice, that character is expressed in the dealings of God with men. There are things that may be said in the consideration of the righteousness and justice of God. First, there is the imposing of righteousness, laws, and demands, which may be called legislative holiness and may be known as the righteousness of God.

Second, there is the executing of the penalties attached to those laws, which may be called judicial holiness. Third, there is the sense in which the attributes of the righteousness and justice of God may be regarded as the actual carrying out of the holy nature of God in the government of the world. W. Evans states:

> Therefore, in the righteousness of God we
> have His love of holiness and in the justice of
> God, His hatred of sin. Again righteousness, as
> here used, has reference to the very nature of God
> as He is in Himself. That attribute which leads
> God always to do right.[30]

Psalm 116:5 tells us, "Gracious is the Lord, and righteousness; yea, our God is merciful." The text shows that it is because of this fact

---

[30] W. Evans, *The Great Doctrines of the Bible*, 40–41.

that God listens to men, and because, having promised to hear, he is bound to keep his promises. Ezra 9:15 declares, "O Lord God of Israel, thou are righteous." The righteousness of Jehovah is acknowledged in the punishment of Israel's sins. Thou are just, thou hast brought us to the state in which we are today. Psalm 145:17 says, "The Lord is righteous in all his ways, and holy in all his works." This is evident in the rewards he gives to the upright and true. Jeremiah 12:1 also tells, "Righteous are thou, O Lord, when I plead with thee I should not be able to convict thee of injustice, even though I be painfully exercised over the mysteries of Thy providence."

These scriptures clearly set forth not only the fact that God is righteous and just, but also define these attributes. Here, we are told that God, in his government of the world, does always that which is suitable, straight, and right. W. Evans states:

> The righteousness and justice of God are revealed in two ways. Frist, in punishing the wicked-retributive justice; and second, in rewarding the righteous remunerative justice.[31]

In reference to the punishment of the wicked, Psalm 11:4–6 declares:

> The LORD is in his Holy temple, The Lord's throne is in heaven: his eyes behold, his eyelids try, the children of men.
> The LORD trieth the righteous; but the wicked and him that loveth violence his soul hateth.
> Upon the wicked he shall rain snares, fire and brimstone and an horrible tempest. This shall be the portion of their cup.

This is David's reply to his timid advisers. Saul may reign upon the earth and do wickedly, but God reigns from heaven and will do

---

[31] W. Evans, *The Great Doctrines of the Bible*, 41–42.

right. He sees who does right and who does wrong. There is that in his nature which recoils from the evil that he sees and will lead him ultimately to punish it. There is such thing as the wrath of God, and it is described in Psalm 11:4–6. Whatever awful thing the description in this verse may mean for the wicked, God grant that we may never know.

In Exodus 9:23–26, we have the account of the plague of hail. After which come the words "And Pharaoh sent for Moses and Aaron, and said unto them, I have sinned this time: the Lord is righteous, and I and my people are wicked" (Exodus 9:27). Here, Pharaoh acknowledges the perfect justice of God in punishing him for his sin and rebellion. He knew that he had deserved it all, even though cavilers today say there was injustice with God in his treatment of Pharaoh. Pharaoh himself certainly did not think so. Daniel 9:12–14 and Revelation 16:5–6 bring out the same thought. How careful sinners ought to be to fall into the hands of the righteous Judge!

Regarding forgiving the sins of the penitent, 1 John 1:9 tells us, "If we confess our sins, he is faithful and just to forgive us our sins, and to cleanse us from all unrighteousness." Ordinarily, the forgiveness of sin is associated with the mercy, love, and compassion of God, and not with his righteousness and justice. This verse assures us that if we confess our sins, the righteousness and justice of God are our guarantee for forgiveness; but God can forgive us from all sins.

In keeping his word and promise to his children, Nehemiah 9:7 says, "Thou art the Lord the God, who didst choose Abram…and made a covenant with him to give the land of the Canaanites…to his seed, and hast performed thy words; for thou are righteous."

We need to recall the tremendous obstacles which stood in the way of the fulfillment of this promise, and yet we should remember the eleventh chapter of Hebrews. When God gives his word and makes a promise—whether in heaven, on earth, or in hell—he can make that promise void. His righteousness is the guarantee of its fulfillment.

In showing himself to be vindicator of his people from all their enemies, Psalm 129:1–4 states, "Many a time have they afflicted me…yet they have not prevailed against me. The Lord is righteous: he hath cut asunder the cords of the wicked." Sooner or later, God's people will triumph gloriously as David triumphed over Saul. Even in this life, God will give us rest from our enemies, and there shall assuredly come a day when we shall be where the wicked cease from troubling and the weary are at rest.

The Bible speaks frankly about the rewarding of the righteous. Hebrews 6:10 assures us, "For God is not unrighteous to forget your work and labor of love, which ye have shewed toward his name, in that ye have ministered to the saints, and do minister." Those who had shown their faith by their works would not now be allowed to lose that faith.

The very idea of divine justice implies that the use of this grace, thus evidenced, will be rewarded, not only by continuance in grace, but in their final perseverance and reward. Two Timothy 4:8 tells us, "Henceforth there is laid up for me a crown of righteousness, which the Lord the righteous judge, will give me at that day: and not to me only, but unto all them also that love his appearing." W. Evans states:

> The righteous Judge will not allow the faithful believer to go unrewarded. He is not like the unrighteous judges of Rome and the Athenian games. Here we are not always rewarded, but some time we shall receive full reward for all the good that we have done. The righteousness of God is the guarantee of all this.[32]

When acknowledging the attributes of God, his mercy and loving-kindness must be mentioned. In general, these attributes mean kindness, goodness, and compassion of God. It deals with the love of God in its relation to both the obedient and the disobedient sons of men. More specifically, mercy is usually exercised in connection with guilt. It is that attribute of God which leads him to seek the welfare,

---

[32] W. Evans, *The Great Doctrines of the Bible*, 42–43.

both temporal and spiritual, of sinners, even at the cost of great sacrifice on his part.

> But God, who is rich in mercy, for his great
> love wherewith he loves us… God commendeth his
> love towards us, in that, while we were yet sinners,
> Christ died for us. (Ephesians 2:4; Romans 5:8)

Loving-kindness is that attribute of God which leads him to bestow upon his obedient children his constant and choice blessing.

> "He that spared not his own Son, but freely
> delivered him up for us all, how shall "he" not
> with him freely give us all things?" (Romans 8:32)

There are various scriptures which support these facts. Psalm 103:8 declares, "The Lord is merciful and gracious, slow to anger, and plenteous in mercy." For, instead of inflicting pain, poverty, and death, which are the wages of sin, God has spared our lives, given us health, and increased our blessings and comforts. Deuteronomy 4:31 states, "(For the LORD thy God is a merciful God); he will not forsake thee, neither destroy thee, nor forget the covenant of thy fathers which he sware unto them."

God is ready to accept the penitence of Israel, even now, if only it is sincere. Israel will return and find God only because he is merciful and does not let go of her. It is his mercy that forbids him from permanently forsaking his people. Psalm 86:15 supports this idea: "But thou, O Lord, art a God full of compassion, and gracious, long-suffering, and plenteous in mercy and truth." It was because God had so declared himself to be of this nature that David felt justified in feeling that God would not utterly forsake him in his time of great stress and need.

The most striking illustration of the mercy and loving-kindness of God is set forth in the parable of the prodigal son (Luke 15:11–32). Here, we have not only the welcome awaiting the wanderer, but also the longing for his return on the part of the anxious and loving father. W. Evans states:

> It is important to note the manifestation of God' mercy and loving-kindness. In general, we must not forget that God is absolutely sovereign in the bestowal of His blessings. "Therefore hath he mercy on whom he will have mercy" (Romans 9:18). We should also remember that God wills to have mercy on all His Creatures, "For thou, Lord, are good, and ready to forgive, and plenteous in mercy to all them that call upon thee" (Psalm 86:5).[33]

God does extend mercy towards sinners in particular. Luke 6:36 exhorts, "Be ye therefore merciful, as your Father also merciful."

> That ye may be the children of your Father which is in heaven: for he maketh his sun to rise on the evil and on the good, and sendeth rain on the just and on the unjust. (Matthew 5:45)

Here, even the impenitent and hard-hearted are recipients of God's mercy. All sinners, even the impenitent, are included in the sweep of his mercy. Isaiah 55:7 notes, "Let the wicked forsake his way, and the unrighteous man his thoughts: and let him return unto the Lord, and he will have mercy upon him; and to our God, for he will abundantly pardon."

God's mercy is a holy mercy; it will, by no means, protect sin but anxiously awaits to pardon it. God's mercy is a city of refuge for the penitent, but by no means a sanctuary for the presumptuous (see Proverbs 28:13 and Psalm 51:1). God's mercy is here seen in pardoning the sin of those who do truly repent.

---

[33] W. Evans, *The Great Doctrines of the Bible*, 44.

We speak about "trusting in the mercy of the Lord." Let us forsake sin and then trust in the mercy of the Lord, and we shall find pardon. Two Peter 3:9 tells us, "The Lord…is long-suffering to us-ward, not willing that any should perish, but that all should come to repentance." Nehemiah 9:31 supports this attribute, "Nevertheless for thy great mercies' sake thou didst not utterly consume them, for thou are a gracious and merciful God." Here is mercy manifested in forbearance with sinners.

If God should have dealt with them in justice, they would have been cut off long before. Think of the evil, the impurity, and the sin that God must see. How it must disgust him. Then remember that he could crush it all in a moment. Yet, he does not. He pleads; he sacrifices to show his love for sinners. Surely, it is because of the Lord's mercies that we are not consumed and because his compassions fail not. Yet, beware lest we abuse this goodness for our God is also a consuming fire. The mercy of God is here shown in His loving forbearance with sinners. W. Evans states:

> In addition, God extends loving-kindness to the saints, Psalm 32:10 in particular states, "But he that trusted in the Lord, mercy shall compass him about." The very act of trust on the part of the believer moves the heart of God to protect him just as in the case of a parent and his child. The moment I throw myself on God I am enveloped in His mercy. Mercy is my environment, like a fiery wall it surrounds me, without a break through which an evil can creep. Resistance surrounds us with "sorrow" but trust surrounds us with "mercy." In the center of that circle of mercy sits and rests the trusting soul.[34]

Philippians 2:27 tells us, "For indeed he was sick nigh unto death: but God had mercy on him; and not on him only, but on

---

[34] W. Evans, *The Great Doctrines of the Bible*, 45–46.

me also, lest I should have sorrow upon sorrow." Here, God's loving kindness is seen healing his sick children. Yet, remember that he hath mercy on whom he will have mercy.

Not every sick child of God is raised. In Psalm 7:2–4, the Psalmist cries, "Have mercy upon me, O Lord, for I am weak: O Lord, heal, me… Deliver my soul for thy mercies sake." The Psalmist asks God to illustrate his mercy in restoring to him his spiritual health. From these scriptures, we see that the mercy of God is revealed in healing his children of bodily and spiritual sickness. W. Evans states:

> This is also illustrated in Psalm 21:7: "For the king trusteth in the Lord, and through the mercy of the most High he shall not be moved." David feels that, because he trusts in the mercy of the Lord, his throne, whatever may dash against it, is perfectly secure. Is not this true also of the believer's eternal security? More to the mercy of God than to the perseverance of the saints is to be attributed the eternal security of the believer. "He will hold me fast."[35]

The love of God, in reference to Christianity, is really the only religion that sets forth the Supreme Being as love. The gods of the heathen are angry, hateful beings, and are in constant need of appeasing. In support of this fact, 1 John 4:8–16 declares, "God is love"… "God is light"… "God is Spirit"… "God is love." Spirit and light are expressions of God's essential nature. Love is the expression of his personality corresponding of his nature. It is the nature of God to love. He dwells always in the atmosphere of love. Just how to define or describe the love of God may be difficult, if not impossible. It appears in certain scriptures (1 John 3:16 and John 3:16) that the love of God is of such a nature that it betokens a constant interest on the physical and spiritual welfare of his creatures as to lead him to make sacrifices beyond human conception to reveal that love.

---

[35] W. Evans, *The Great Doctrines of the Bible*, 46.

The object of God's love is especially displayed concerning Jesus Christ, his only begotten Son. In Matthew 3:17, God declares, "This is my beloved Son, in whom I am well pleased" (see also Matthew 17:5 and Luke 20:13). In verse 19 of the third chapter of Matthew, Jesus Christ shares the love of the Father in a unique sense, just as he is his Son in a unique sense. He is especially "My chosen," "The one in whom my soul delighteth," and "My beloved Son."

Thus, literally, the Son of mine, the beloved. And we can readily understand how he, who did the will of God perfectly, should, thus, become the special object of the Father's love. Of course, if the love of God is eternal, as is the nature of God, which must be the case then that love must have had an eternal object to love. So Christ, in addressing the Father, says, "Thou lovedst me before the foundation of the world".(John 17:24).

Those who are believers in God's Son, Jesus Christ, are special objects of God's love. John 16:27 states, "For the Father himself loveth you, because ye have loved me, and have believed that I came out from God." An example of this is found in John 14:21–23, which states:

> He that hath my commandments, and keepeth them, he it is that loveth me: and he that loveth me shall be loved of my Father, and I will love him, and will manifest myself to him.
>
> Judas saith unto him, not Iscariot, Lord, how is it that thou wilt manifest thyself unto us, and not unto the world?
>
> Jesus answered and said unto him, if a man love me, he will keep my words: and my Father will love him, and we will come unto him, and make our abode with him.

Do we really believe these words? We are not on the outskirts of God's love, but in its very midst. Christ stands right in the very midst of that circle of the Father's love. Then he draws us to that spot and, as it were, disappears, leaving us standing there bathed in the same loving-kindness of the Father, in which he himself had basked.

Does God love the world of sinners and ungodly men? John 3:16 declared, "For God so loved the world." To Nicodemus, in his narrow exclusivism, it was a startling truth. God loved not only the Jew, but also the Gentile; not simply a part of the world of men, but every man in it, irrespective of his moral character. For "God commendeth his love towards us, in that, while we were yet sinners, Christ died for us" (Romans 5:8). The love of God is broader than the measure of man's mind. God desires the salvation of all men (1 Timothy 2:4).

How does the love of God reveal itself? By making infinite sacrifice for the salvation of men. In 1 John 4:9–10, it says:

> In this was manifested the love of God towards us, because that God sent His only begotten Son into the world, that we might live through him.
>
> Herein is love, not that we loved God, but that God loved us, and sent His Son to be the propitiation for our sins.

Love is more than compassion; it hides not itself as compassion may but displays itself actively on behalf of its object. The Cross of Calvary is the higher expression of the love of God for sinful men. He gave not only a Son, but His only Son—his well-beloved.

In bestowing full and complete pardon on the penitent, Isaiah 38:17 tells us, "Thou hast sins behind thy back." Literally, "Thou hast loved my soul back from the pit of destruction." God had taken the bitterness out of his life and given him the gracious forgiveness of his sins but putting them far away from him.

Ephesians 2:4–5 says, "But God, who is rich in mercy, for his great love wherewith he loved us, Even when we were dead in sins, hath quickened us together with Christ." Verses 1–3 of this chapter show the destruction of the race into ruin. *But* reverses the picture when all help for man fails. Then God steps in, and by his mercy, which springs from *his great love*, redeems fallen man and gives him not only pardon, but a position in his heavenly kingdom by the side of Jesus Christ.

In remembering his children in all the varying circumstances of life, Isaiah 63:9 says, "In all their affliction he was afflicted, and the angel of his presence saved them: in his love and in his pity he redeemed them; and he bare them, and carried them all the days of old." Here is retrospection on the part of the prophet. He thinks of all the oppression of Israel and recalls how God's interests have been bound up with theirs. He was not their adversary—he was their sympathetic, loving friend. He suffered with them.

Isaiah 49:15–16 states, "Can a woman forget her sucking child… Yea, they may forget, yet will I not forget thee. Behold, I have engraved thee on the palms of my hands; thy walls are continually before me."

Absolute Imminent Attributes

1st Division: Spirituality

God is invisible, incorporeal, without parts, without body, without passion, and, therefore, free from all limitations. He is apprehended not by the senses, but by the soul. Hence, God is above sensual perception. One Corinthians 2:6–16 intimates that without the teaching of God's Spirit, we cannot know God. He is not a material Being. W. Evans states:

> La Place swept the heavens with his telescope, but he could not find anywhere a God. He might just as well have swept a kitchen with his broom. Since God is not a material Being, He cannot be apprehended by physical means.[36]

2nd Division: Infinity

Infinity is a term used in mathematics. It is derived from the theory of sets propounded by the German mathematician George Cantor. The New Encyclopedia states:

> Sets may be divided into two classes, depending on whether or not their elements

---

[36] W. Evans, *The Great Doctrines of the Bible*, 19.

can be put into a one-to-one correspondence (matched in a one-to-one way) with the elements of some proper subset. A set "A" is a proper subset of a set "B" if every element of "A" belongs to "B", but "B" has at least one element that does not belong to "A". The elements of the set (1, 2, 3) cannot be matched in a one-to-one way with the elements of any one of its proper subsets; such a set is called a finite set. The elements of the set (2, 4, 6,…2n,…) can be matched in a one-to-one way with the elements of the proper subset (6, 8, 10,…2+4…) by matching, for any positive integer, the element 2n of the first set with element 2n=4 the second. Thus, the set n of all positive integers, the set R of all rational numbers, and the set Z of all real numbers are infinite sets. The term "infinite" and "infinity" are used in other related ways. For example, in the infinite sequence], 4, 9,…of which the Nth term, a n, becomes infinite as n becomes infinite, meaning that a n is larger than any arbitrary preassigned number if n is large then a certain value.[37]

3rd Division: Perfection

The definition of the word *perfection*, whose basic meaning is closest to the fundamental etymological sense of the English word *complete* or *finished*, is used for the ritually clean victims of sacrifice (Exodus 12:5) and uprightness of character (Genesis 6:9, 17:1 and Psalm 119:1).

The New Testament suggests that *perfection* is an attainment of the end or aims of being and is therefore a relative term to be understood within its context. *Absolute* can therefore be an attribute of God

---

[37] Funk & Wagnalls New Encyclopedia, Vol. 13, p. 290–291.

alone. Hence, the explanation found in Philippians 3:12, 15 and Matthew 5:48 commands perfection—it involves no impossibility.

The word *perfect*, as the Bible uses it of man, does not refer to sinless perfection. The Old Testament characters described as *perfect* were obviously not sinless (Genesis 6:9, 1 King 15:4, 2 King 20:3, Job 1:18, and Psalm 37:37). Although a number of Hebrew and Greek words are translated *perfect*, the thought is usually *completeness in all details* (Hebrew: *tamamam*; Greek: *katartizo*) or *to reach a goal or achieve a purpose* (Greek: *telacoo*). C. I. Schofield says:

> The Christian is enjoined to fulfill the functions of his being as God fulfills His, and the sermon in which the precept is embedded explains the made and manner of such attainment.[38]

The concept of perfection which has been taught by some theologians and preachers has erred in neglecting the relativity of the term *perfection* and such clear teaching as that of John (1 John 1:8), James (James 3:2), and Paul (Philippians 3:12) scripture references.

John tells us in 1 John 1:8: "If we say that we have no sin, we deceive ourselves, and the truth is not in us." James tells us, "For in many things we offend all. If any man offend not in word, the same is a perfect man, and able to bridle the whole body" (James 3:2). The New Compact Dictionary states:

> The perfection of God by which He is devoid of all change in essence, attributes, consciousness, will, and promise. No change is possible in God, because all change must be for better or worse, and God is absolute perfection.[39]

In Philippians 3:12, Paul says, "Not as though I had already attained, either were already perfect: but I follow after, if that I may

---

[38] C. I. Schofield, The New Schofield Bible: Holy Bible.
[39] New Compact Dictionary, 447.

apprehend that for which also I am apprehended of Christ Jesus." The New Compact Dictionary states:

> There is no cause for change in God, God
> exists either in Himself or outside Himself.[40]

There are three stages of perfection revealed: positional, relative, and ultimate. First, positional perfection already obtained by every believer in Christ (Hebrew 10:14). Second, relative perfection, spiritual maturity (Philippians 3:15), especially in such aspects as the will of God (Colossians 4:12), love (1 John 4:17–18), holiness (1 Corinthians 7:1), patience (James 1:4), and every good work (Hebrew 13:21). Maturity is achieved progressively (1 Corinthians 7:1).

Secondly, perfecting holiness (Galatians 3:3), literally "we are yet now being made perfect," and this is accomplished through the gifts of ministry bestowed "for the perfecting of the saints" (Ephesians 4:12).

Third, ultimate perfection—perfection in soul, body and spirit—which Paul denies he has attained (Philippians 3:12) but will have attained by the time of the resurrection of the dead (Philippians 3:11). For the Christian, nothing is short of the moral perfection. God is always the absolute standard of conduct, but scripture recognizes that Christians do not attain sinless perfection in this life (1 Peter 1:15–16, 1 John 1:8–10).

----

[40] New Compact Dictionary, 446.

Relative Transitive Attributes

Define Relative

The definition for *relative* refers to kindred of some family, related by the same blood and not of the same nature or character, having connection, and properly bearing upon the matter at hand.

Define Transitive

The definition for *transitive* means having, requiring, or terminating upon a direct object; also expressing an action performed by a subject, agent, or that which passes over take effect on some person or thing as its object. It is also having power of passing, effecting transition.

Define Attributes

The definition for *attributes* is inherent in a person, an inseparable property to belonging, ascribed, assigned, associate, change, connect, impute, or refer. A characteristic attribute must express something of the real nature of that which is ascribed. When we speak of the attributes of God, the quality of matter, we simply refer a matter to the cause or class to which it belong or ascribed to, one what is really his. Funk & Wagnalls states:

> When we are quite sure, we simply refer a matter to the cause or class to which it belongs or ascribed to one what is really his. A property is what belongs especially to one as his own peculiar possession, in distinction from all other things; which when we speak of the qualities or properties of matter, quality is the more general, property is the more limited term.[41]

---

[41] Funk & Wagnalls Standard Dictionary, Vol. 1, p. 94.

CHAPTER 3

The Trinity

God the Father

Our God, the Father, has infinite knowledge and wisdom. Our God, the Father, is infinitely present everywhere. Our God, the Father, is infinitely powerful everywhere. Our God, the Father, is infinitely holy, love, grace, and perfection. Our God, the Father, has in infinite number of perfect universes. The name *Elohim*, signifying power, strength, prominence, greatness, and glory, is used 2,570 times in the Old Testament and frequently revealing the great power of God. Genesis opens with the use of this wonderful name in creation of the heaven and the earth.

Another reason the name *God* is plural in the Old Testament. This is the first revelation in the Bible in which God is plural: intimating God; The Father, God the Son, and God the Holy Spirit. This is the Godhead, the Deity, working jointly in the acts of creation (Genesis 1:26). The verbs that follow are always in singular form. This is consistent with the forthcoming revelation in the Bible of the Holy Trinity. The New Schofield Reference Bible states:

> It is significant that the first appearance of
> the name Jehovah in scripture followed the creation of man (Exodus 34:7).[42]

It was God (Elohim) who said, "Let us make man in our own image," (Genesis 1:26); but when man (Genesis chapter 2) is to fill the scene and become dominant over creation, it is the Lord God (Jehovah Elohim) who acts (Genesis 2:4). This clearly indicates a special relation of Deity in his Jehovah personality to man and all

---

[42] C. I. Schofield, *The New Schofield Reference Bible: Holy Bible*, 117.

scripture emphasizing this. Jehovah is distinctly the redemption name of Deity.

When sin entered the world and man's redemption became necessary, it was Jehovah Elohim who sought the sinning ones (Genesis 3:9–13) and clothed them with coats of skins (Genesis 3:21). A beautiful type of the righteousness is provided by the Lord God through sacrifice. The first instinctive revelation of himself by his name Jehovah was in connection with the covenant people out of Egypt. God reveals himself as the Lord. The New Schofield Reference Bible says:

> Moses was commissioned and Moses said unto God, behold, when I come unto the children of Israel, and shall say unto them, the God of your fathers hath sent me, unto you; and they shall say unto me, What is his name? What shall I say unto them? And God said unto Moses, I AM That I AM: and He said, Thus shall thy say unto the children of Israel, I AM hath sent me unto you.
>
> And God said moreover unto Moses, Thus shall thy say unto the children of Israel, The Lord God of your fathers the God of Abraham the God of Isaac, and the God of Jacob, hath sent me unto you; this is my name forever, and this is my memorial unto all generations.
>
> Go, and gather the elders of Israel together and say unto them the Lord God of your father, the God of Abraham, of Isaac, and Jacob, appeared unto me, saying, I have surely visited you, and seen that which is done to you in Egypt.
>
> And I have said I will bring you up out of the affliction of Egypt into the land of Canaanities, Hittites, Amorites, Periszites, Hivites, and Jebusites. (Exodus)[43]

---

[43] C. I. Schofield, The New Schofield Reference Bible: Holy Bible, 73–73.

In Exodus 3:14, in this initial self-identification of God, it is significant that the verb is in the first person; the speaker names himself, thus, emphasizing his personal identification. It is the announcement of a present God, who has come to fulfill his covenant and keep his promise to the afflicted people of Abraham, Isaac, and Jacob.

The mystery and character of God is given to us first from his work and then revealed from his word. Then from his Son and finally, from the Holy Spirit unto the believers' lives. This truly is the definition of God. God is love! His love surpasses illustration, defies comparison, and braggart description. God is light! What light is to the material world, God is the source of light in the spiritual.

God is spirit! The Father of love gave his Son to light a world darkened by sin, and the Holy Spirit glorifies the light of the world, along with works at reproving the world of sin, unrighteousness, and judgment.

GOD THE SON

In the beginning, God created the heaven and the earth. For it is plain in the scriptures that God is, in fact, a Trinity: God the Father, God the Son, God the Holy Spirit. And so it is in the unfolding of the scriptures that we find God the Son (Christ) to whom creation has been ascribed (Colossians 1:17).

The scriptures themselves recognize and tell us that all things are deliberately held together by Christ. In the scriptures before Genesis 2:4, the general term *God* had been used. In verse 4, the name *Jehovah* (Lord) is introduced and continued to be used for several chapters. The documentary theory of the authorship of the Pentateuch was built, in part, on the basis of this change in name of God (Genesis 2:4). For they use *Lord God* instead of *God* as in Genesis 2:5, which states, "For the Lord God had not caused it to rain upon the earth, and there was not a man to till the ground."

The *Lord God* formed man from the dust of the ground and breathed into his nostrils the breath of life, and man became a living soul. And the Lord God planted a garden eastward in Eden, and there he put man whom he had formed.

> And the LORD God said, it is not good that the man be alone; I will make him a help meet for him. (Genesis 2:18)

> And the LORD God caused a deep sleep to fall upon Adam, and he slept: and He took one of his ribs, and closed up the flesh instead thereof; (Genesis 2:21)

The man was created (not evolved) and appeared as the crown and glory of all God's recreative activity with regards to the earth as man's special home. The expression "Let us" in Genesis 1:26 intimates the true God's council and activity in man's creation. Two words do express the same thing and make each other more expressive: *image* and *likeness* denote the *like image*.

Still, between God the Son and man, there is an infinite distance. Christ, God the Son, is only the expressed image of God's person as the Son of the Father having the same nature.

God the Son's image in which man consists in these three things. In his nature and constitution, but not of his body for God has not a body, but a soul. This honor God, indeed, has put upon the man in that the Word was made flesh. The Son was clothed with glory like ours, and God will shortly clothe our bodies with a glory like unto that of his own. But it is the soul, the great soul of man, that does especially bear God the Son's image. The soul of man is considered in three noble faculties: understanding, will, and active power.

Note first that Christ, God the Son, preceded all things, and that all things were made by him. He is thus tied in with purpose for which things have been made. And observe carefully now the last phrase: "And by Him all things consist; consist, cohere, hang together, or bind together for His counsel purpose" (Colossians 1:13–17).

My observation of the question is "How could Christ, God the Son, be able to hold all things together?" The answer is that Christ, God the Son, is the second person in the Deity. Even though He took on human form by physical birth a human body like ours, he never orated his omnipresence. This is why it is possible for him to come and live in all bodies of all his redeemed.

I am grateful, deeply grateful, to Mr. Eli Gaverluk and Mr. Matthew Henry for the great insight they gave me to share with others.

God the Holy Ghost

Ezekiel 36:27 says, "And I will put my spirit in you, and cause you to walk in my statues, and ye shall keep my judgments, and do them." The Holy Spirit comes from God to represent God to the believer, and the Lord goes before God to represent the believer to God. The Holy Spirit becomes our representative of Christ on earth. Christ becomes our representative to God in heaven. The Holy Spirit makes intercession for the believer, and Christ makes intercession for the believer.

Regarding Genesis 1:3, it would be proper undoubtedly, to say that the Father created all things through the agency of the word and the Spirit. In the Genesis account of creation, the Spirit is seen actively engaged in the work of creation. Not only is it true that the Spirit is seen in the act of creation, but his power is seen also in the presentation of nature.

Genesis 1:2 says that God the Holy Spirit was the first to move; he moved upon the face of the waters. The Spirit of God began to work, and if he works, who or what shall hinder? God is said to have made the world by his Spirit (Psalm 33:6), and by the mighty work, the new creation is effected. He moved upon the face of the deep. God is not only the author of all beings, but also the fountain of life.

The Spirit is equal with the Father and the Son in distribution of spiritual gifts. By the Deity of the Holy Spirit is meant that the Holy Spirit is God. But the Holy Spirit and Christ are called by this name the Paraclete, and they are the only Ones in scriptures who have this name. The Holy Spirit comes from God. Christ is the Paraclete (advocate) in heaven, and the Holy Spirit is the Paraclete (comforter) on earth.

For your meditation, I give you the fact that God is three gifts of grace: faith, hope, and love. Faith speaks of our own dependence. Hope speaks of our own life. Love speaks to us of God. Faith is an intimation of God. Love is the manifestation of God. Faith and hope acquire blessings, but love bestows blessings. Before hope and faith, love said, "I am." Love was before works. Love is eternal. Love is the nature and whole of God.

Proofs from the Old Testament

The divine name *God* is a plural word. Plural pronouns are used of God. The Hebrew word for God, *Elohim* is used most frequently in the plural form. God often uses plural pronouns in speaking of himself as seen in Genesis 1:26: "Let us make man;" Isaiah 6:8: "Who will go for us;" and Genesis 3:22: "Behold, man is become one of us." The "us" of Genesis 1:26 is properly understood as plural majesty, indicating the dignity and majesty of the speaker. The proper translation of this verse should not be "Let us make man" but "we will make man." This indicates the language of resolve rather than consultation.

The doctrine of the unity of God does not exclude the plurality of persons in Godhead. There are not three personalities in each person of the Godhead. I believe, therefore, that there are three persons in the Godhead but one God. The scriptures assert the unity of God: Deuteronomy 6:4 says, "Hear O Israel; the Lord our God is one Lord" (or the Lord our God). Isaiah 44:6–8 says, "I am the first, and I am the last, and beside me there is no God… Is there a God beside me? There is no God; I know not any." Isaiah 48:12 says, "Hearken unto me, O Jacob and Israel, my called: I am he; I am the first, I am also the last."

Isaiah 48:16 says, "Come ye near unto me, hear ye this: I have not spoken in secret from the beginning; from the time that it was, there am I: and now the Lord God, and His spirit has sent me". This is one of the clearest of the Old Testament intimations of the Trinity. For the speaker here is not the prophet but the Lord himself.

Isaiah 46:5 tells us, "To whom will ye liken me, and make me equal, and compare me that we may be a like."

Isaiah 46:9 says, "Remember the former things of old; for I am God, and there is none like me."

There is but one self-existent being. The Bible reveals God to us as the one and only God. There cannot be more than one God for eternity, infinity, and omnipresence, and almighty cannot apply to more than one such being. Two such beings would limit and exclude each other and thus render impossible the being of God. God makes himself known in the scriptures as Father, Son, and Holy Ghost. In Genesis 1:26, there aren't three separate persons, but three personalities in the Godhead.

Intimations from the Old Testament

Intimation is a declaration or notification and also information communicated indirectly—a hint.

The Old Testament saints knew about the resurrection of the dead. Isaiah 26:19 says, "Thy dead man shall live, together with my dead body shall they arise. Awake, and sing, ye that dwell in dust… the earth shall cast out the dead." Daniel 12:2 declares, "And many of them that sleep in the dust of the earth shall awake."

In Job 14:14, Job asked the question, "If a man die shall he live again? All the days of my appointed time will I wait till my change come." In Job 19:25–27, it says:

> For I know that my redeemer liveth, and
> that he shall stand at the latter day upon the earth.
> And though after my skin worms destroy
> this body, yet in my flesh shall I see God.
> Whom I shall see for myself and not another;
> though my reins be consumed within me.

In Job 19:26, this passage contains one of the most sublime expressions in the Old Testament of faith in the living Redeemer. His Personal appearance on earth and the participation of the godly in the resurrection of bliss because of Him and the assured vision of God by the righteous (Job 14:13–15).

Isaiah 25:8–9 notes:

> He will swallow up death in victory; and the Lord God will wipe away tears from all faces; and the rebuke of his people, shall he take away from off all the earth: for the Lord hath spoken it.
>
> And it shall be said in that day, Lo, this is our God; we have waited for him, and he will save us: this is the Lord: we have waited for him, we will be glad and rejoice in His salvation.

Genesis 5:24 says, "And Enoch walked with God: and he was not; for God took him." In 2 Kings 2:11, Elijah and Elisha went on and behold a chariot of fire, and of horses departed them; and Elijah went up by a whirlwind into heaven. Elijah is carried up to heaven in a fiery chariot, and like Enoch, he was translated that he should not see death and was not. Mr. Cawley expressed:

> The second man that leaped the ditch, where all the rest of mankind fell, and went not downward to the sky.[44]

Relation of Persons in Trinity of Each Other

The hymnal says:

> Father in heaven, whose love profound. A ransom for our souls hath found, before thy throne we sinner bend; to me thy parting love extend. Almighty Son, incarnated word my Prophet, Priest, Redeemer, and Lord, before thy throne we sinners bend; to me thy saving grace please extend. External spirit whose breath my

---

[44] Lawrence O. Richards, *The Teacher's Commentary*, 312–316.

soul, is raised from sin, and death, before thy throne we sinners bend; to me thy quicking power extend. Jehovah! Father, Holy Spirit, Son mysterious Godhead three in one, before thy throne me, a sinner bend; grace, pardon, and the life to me extend, please Holy Trinity.

With three, we come to the number of union, approval, approbation, coordination, completeness, and perfection. It is the number of the Trinity. Three persons in one God, three members of divine perfection.

In Isaiah 6, the Seraphim, praising God, said, "Holy, Holy, Holy." It is significant that they stopped at three. But these beings were declaring the tri-unity of God. We speak often of distinction in the Godhead. The Doctrine of the Trinity in the Old Testament is not so much declared as intermitted in the Old Testament. The burden of the Old Testament's message seems to be the unity of God.

Yet the doctrine of the Trinity is clearly intermitted through the plural noun *Elohim*, and the plural pronouns *us* and *our*. In Genesis 1:26, it says, "And God said, Let us make in our image and after our likeness." A declaration is made in the New Testament where only an intimation is made in the Old Testament.

At the baptism of Jesus, we have all three persons present. Note in Matthew 3:16–17: The Lord Jesus was in the water, the Father spoke from heaven saying: "This is my beloved Son in whom I am well pleased." And the Holy Ghost (Spirit) came from heaven to earth in the form of a dove, lighting upon him. Perhaps, we should say that this is a threefold personality.

A little girl once said, "Three in one, and one in three, and the one in the middle stands for me." (We should go to the children more for simple definitions). This is the mystery, which no human being can really explain.

The Trinity is intimated in a threefold way. First, the plural nouns of Deity *Elohim*. Second, the personal pronoun used of the Deity. Third, the Theophanies, specially the "Angel of the Lord."

The New Testament is the outgrowth of the Old Testament. "The Old" is the root, and "The New" is the shoot. "The New" is in "The Old" contained, and "The Old is in "The New" explained. The Old Testament is filled with prophecies concerning Christ, which are fulfilled and explained in the New Testament. The very first verse of the New Testament links up the "The Old." The prophecies concerning Jesus Christ, which are recorded in the Old Testament, may be classified under four headings:

1. Kings—Psalm 2:6; Isaiah 32:1, Daniel 9:25
2. Servant—Isaiah 2:1; 52:13
3. Son of Man—Isaiah 7:12; 9:6–7; Daniel 7:13–14
4. Son of God—Isaiah 9:6–7; 40:3–9

Christ is set forth in the Old Testament as the *branch*, and the Old Testament provides names:

1. Jeremiah 23:5—"The Branch King"—the Lion
2. Zechariah 3:8—"The Branch"—the Servant
3. Zachariah 6:12—"The Branch"—the Man
4. Isaiah 4:2—"The Branch of the Lord"—the Eagle

Don't live in the Old Testament only nor in the New Testament alone, but in the whole word of God. The Old Testament is the kindergarten, and when we have finished with the kindergarten, we go on into the "University of Scripture." We must have the Old Testament in order to understand the New Testament. You must know who David and Abraham were. We have Leviticus in order to understand the book of Hebrew. You must have the whole word of God.

CHAPTER 4

The Decrees of God

The decrees of God are ordinances edited by judicial decisions or orders. A decree of God is one of the eternal purposes of God, by which events are foreordained or decided by decree of a formal order, determining what is to be done or not done to a particular matter.

The golden image and the king's decree was a plot. For Daniel 2:9 states, "But if you will not make known unto me the dream, there is but one decree, for you…the king's decree." Daniel 2:13 states, "And the decree went forth that the wise men should be slain; and they sought Daniel and his fellows to be slain."

In Daniel 2:19, the secret was revealed unto Daniel in a night vision. Daniel blessed the God of heaven; God can change things, and he can change people. In Daniel 3:29, God did change the king's heart, and he made a new decree saying:

Therefore, I make a decree, That every people, nation, and language, which speak anything amiss the God of Shadrach, Meshach, and Abednego, shall be cut in pieces, and their houses shall be made a dunghill: because there is no other God that can deliver after this sort.

Psalm 2:7 begins with, "I will declare the decree." This is the climax of the second Psalms. There is a decree of God; it is folly to resist. What is the decree? That God has sent his own Son to Zion as king over all the earth. That the decree is made known to keep the world's heart from fainting. The first promise broken through the darkness of the fall, but of ultimate triumph on the part of the redeemer. And He, who, of foretime has been known as the seed of the woman, the seed of Abraham, the Shiloh who blessed expiring Jacob, the Angel of the covenant, the Divine Prophet, is now revealed in all his majesty and renown as the brightness of the Father's glory. The hymnal states:

> Whatever my God ordained is right: He never will deceive me; He leads me by the proper path; I know he will not leave me; I take content, what he hath sent; His hand can turn my grief away, and patiently I will wait this day.
>
> Whatever my God ordained is right: though now this cup I am drinking, may seem bitter to my fainting heart in I take it surely my God is true; each morning and new; Sweet comfort yet shall fill my heart, and pain and sorrow shall depart. Because, I know that whatever my God ordained is surely right.[45]

---

[45] J. Montgomery, *Trinity Hymnal*, 94.

Definition is the action of defining an exact statement of meaning, notice, or limits of some things, clearness of shape, color, or sound. *Definition* is a concise statement or explanation of exact meaning of a word or phrase, the capacity for forming an image of sharp detail.

Statement:

The sound of your radio is perfectly clear to my ears; it certainly gives good definition. Job 19:25–27 states:

> For I know that my redeemer liveth, and
> that he shall stand at the later day upon the earth:
> And though after my skin worms destroy
> this body, yet in my flesh shall I see God;
> Whom I shall see for myself and mine eyes
> shall behold, …and not another; …Though my
> reins be consumed within me.

Isaiah 47:4 states, "As for our redeemer, the LORD of hosts is His name, the Holy One of Israel." Paul says, "I know whom I have believed, and am persuaded that He is able to keep that which I have committed unto him against that day," (2 Timothy 1:12).

Statement:

> For God hath not given us the spirit of fear: but of power, love, and of a sound mind. (2 Timothy 1:7)

Amen. Praise, God.

The definition of *objection* is that which resents and objects, without any adverse or specific reason or feeling of criticism.

Leviticus 18:1–30 relates to the relationship and walk of God's earthly people and his laws regulating the personal relationship of the redeemed. Leviticus 18:1–9 states:

> "And the LORD spake unto Moses, saying,
>
> Speak unto all the congregation of the children of Israel, and say unto them, Ye shall be holy: for I the LORD your God am Holy.
>
> Ye shall fear every man his mother, and his father, and keep my Sabbaths: I am the LORD your God.
>
> Turn ye not unto idols, nor make to yourselves molten gods. I am the LORD your God.
>
> And if ye offer a sacrifice of peace-offerings unto the Lord, ye shall offer it at your own will.
>
> It shall be eaten the same day ye offer it, and on the morrow: and if ought remain until the third day, it shall be burnt in the fire.
>
> And if it be eaten at all on the third day, it is abominable; it shall not be accepted.
>
> Therefore every one that eateth it shall bear his iniquity, because he hath profaned the hallowed thing of the LORD: and that soul shall be cut from among his people.
>
> And when ye reap the harvest of your land, thou shalt not wholly reap the corners of thy

field, neither shalt thou gather the gleanings of
thy harvest.

The entire chapter of Leviticus 18 consists of God's objections
to unlawful marriages and immortalities.

Genesis 1:1 says, "In the beginning God created the heaven and the earth." God is also creator of the universe and man. This verse contains vital truth.

The universe did not exist from eternity nor was it made from existing matter. It did not proceed as an emanation from the infinite but was summoned into being by the decree of God. Science, disclosing to us the marvelous power and accuracy of natural law, compels us to believe in a superintending intelligence who is infinite.

Creation

The existing of the universe by Deity; an act of the original being of God creating the world, the universe and creatures collectively.

Genesis 1:1 and 1:2 are united. These two verses must not be separated. They form an introduction to activity of the seven days (Genesis 1:3, 2:3) because they tell us of the conditions of the earth when God began to make or refashion it.

It "was" (because) wasteness, emptiness, with darkness upon the surface of the chaotic mass. However, the Spirit of God was brooding over the waters. This shows that God had not utterly forsaken nor forgotten the earth, which was ruined by sin at the former angelic inhabitants (Genesis 6:1, Isaiah 14:13–14, Ezekiel 28:12–15).

God yet at work, provided man a companion (Genesis 3:18–22). The Lord God declared that a sexless or unisexual race would not be good and enunciated His purpose to create "a help suitable to man to be in his presence—a help meet for him." Adam named the animals and birds. But these, though companions in a sense, were not help meets on the same physical level as himself. That is why God made a help meet to be a companion for him.

God rested from his work of Genesis chapter 1. On the seventh day, this Sabbath rest of God became the basic of the Mosaic Sabbath (Exodus 20:11). Within the seven days, God recreated the chaotic earth (Genesis 1:3–5). God's creations and the day of each creation are as follows:

The First Day: Light (verses 3–4)
The Second Day: Firmament (verses 6–8)
The Third Day: Land, sea, and plants (verses 9–13)
The Fourth Day: Sun, moon, and stars (verses 14–19)
The Fifth Day: Sea life and birds (verse 13).
The Sixth Day: Land life and man (verse 26).
Man was created, not evolved (verse 31).

When sin first entered the world, the universe, God gave the first intimation (hint) that he would deal with it in mercy as well as in judgment (Genesis 3:15). Heaven and earth were created in the beginning (Genesis 1:1). Two Peter 3:6 says, "Whereby the world that then was, being overflowed with water, perished." There is no date, information, or calendar for the original creation. We must distinguish between create and make. Out of nothing by the power of his word, heaven and earth were created. This is an appeal to faith, not reason. Reason can never discover who God is. God reaches our reason through our faith, and not our faith through our reason.

And the earth was without form, and void; and darkness was upon the face of the deep. And the spirit of God moved upon the face of the waters. (Genesis 1:2)

Isaiah 45:18 says, "For this said the Lord that created the heavens; God himself that formed the earth and made it; He hath established it, He created it not in vain, He formed it to be inhabited: I am the Lord: and there is none else."

I thank God for his incarnated word, his written word, and his spoken word. The word, ministry, and character of God are given from his work, then his Son, and finally from the Holy Spirit in believers' lives. There is a sense in which the creator of the universe may be ascribed to God's spirit. Psalm 33:6 says, "By the word of the Lord were the heavens made; and all the host of them by the breath (spirit) of his mouth."

Preservation

Consider carefully the words of preservation of the Jewish people (race). Other nations have passed away having lost their identity. The Jews remain the generation (race) that has not yet passed away nor will it till all these prophecies be fulfilled (Psalm 22:30, 24:6).

God sends the sunshine and rain. He sends the harvest of golden grain. He is my friend, the main source of my survival and salvation; therefore, I am preserved.

> Thou preparest a table before me in the presence of my enemies: thou anointest my head with oil; my cup runneth over. Surely goodness and mercy shall follow me all the days of my life: and I will dwell in the house of the Lord forever. (Psalm 23:5–6)

In 1 Thessalonians 5:23, it says, "And the very God of peace Himself sanctify you (wholly); and may your spirit and soul, and body be preserved complete, without blame at the coming of our Lord Jesus Christ."

Job 2:4 reads regarding self-preservation: "and Satan answered the Lord, and said, Skin for skin; yea, all that a man hath will he give for his life." For the love of life is not only an instinctive principle, but also, within certain times, to be presently defined to a positive deity.

The precept "Thou shall not kill" refers to myself as well as to my neighbors (Psalm 23:5–6) and requires me to use all lawful means for the preservation of my own life as well as the lives of others.

C. I. Scofield states:

> Instinctively cling to life, it's our duty to use all proper means for its preservation.
> Jude 1–2, is a salutation and address to the believers in general, citing their election their preservation, and their status as "beloved in God the father."[46]

Providence

This word *providence* is not in the Bible. But the doctrine that God is in full control of all events is taught and illustrated fully in the book of Esther. This is the Christian doctrine of providence: the conviction is that the God of the Bible is in full control of the delights of life.

The book of Esther is unusual; in it, God is not mentioned. Yet, again and again, the story shows our sovereign God working quietly behind the scenes, shaping events so that his good purpose for his people is achieved. God cares for us. His foreseeing eye, guardianship over us, and the manifestation of his divine inclination, prove to me that God cares and provides for all of his creatures that he has made.

Another important contribution of Esther is documentation too. What happened to the Jews who did not return to Judah? Esther 3:8 shows that they had scattered throughout the empire, "among the people in all province" of the empire and there kept "themselves separate."

Esther was an orphan girl, brought up in the home of her cousin, Mordecai. As a young woman, Esther was presented to the palace as a candidate to replace the disposed queen of Xerxes. She was pleasant as well as beautiful. She became a favorite of the eunuch in charge of the king's harem. He advised Esther, and following his advice, she pleased the king more than the others. As a result, Xerxes made Esther queen and proclaimed a holiday throughout the empire.

---

[46] The New Schofield Reference Bible: Holy Bible, C. I. Scofield, p. 1349

Mordecai urged Esther to go to the king and beg for her people saying, "Do not think that because you are in the king's house, you alone of all the Jews will escape. For if you remain silent at this time, relief and deliverance for the Jews will arise from another place, but you and your father's family will perish" (Esther 4:13–16).

It must have been difficult for Esther when suddenly the fate of her people appeared to depend on her, taking responsibility and acting with strength and initiative. Esther finally decided to go. She asked Mordecai to have all the Jews fast for her, and for three days, she and her staff would fast too. Then she would risk going to the king, even though it was against the law. And she added, "If I perish, I perish" (Esther 4:16).

To the ancient Greeks, the flow of cause and effect seemed grimmer. The greed tended to fix on tragedy and believed in a mindless "fate" that ruined the hopes of people, no matter what they did. It was still all chance, not good luck, but bad luck. And there was nothing a person could really do to affect those things that influenced and shaped his life. But in the book of Esther, we see another view. The God of miracles, who has at times, intervened in obvious supernatural acts to benefit his people. He is at work in the flow of natural events as well.

God superintends the "chance" experiences that prove to be the turning point in the lives of individuals and in the history of nations. All these things and especially the timing of the events led "naturally" to another, each turning point channeled history to the end. The Jewish people were saved. Lawrence O. Richards states:

> As we look at the Book of Esther, we can see a number of turning points: and events on which the story and its resolution hinge. We can see in effect God setting the stage for happenings that led to the deliverance of His people, the Jews. Events in the Book of Esther are set in era of Persian Empire, sometime; between 483 and 471 BC. Xerxes the great ruled: the same Xerxes invaded Greece, but was thrown back.

Chronologically, the Book of Esther comes between the return of the first group of Jews to Judah from Babylon (538 BC) and the return of a second group led by Ezras event (458 BC) are not set in Babylon but at Susa, which laid close to the Persian Gulf." Archeologist have not discovered documents that mention Esther or her cousin, Mordecai. But the detailed description of Persian court practices and customs in the Book of Esther have been shown to be completely accurate.[47]

---

[47] Lawrence O. Richards, *The Teachers Commentary*, 312–316.

In Mordecai's action toward Haman and the seventy-nine decrees of the kings, two possible conclusions can be drawn here. Perhaps Mordecai's pride should be blamed for his action, of which pleased all of his people in danger of death.

Many events in our world flow directly from human sinfulness while God was in all things. Mordecai need not be held responsible for his willful human actions (Esther 3:1–2).

Another conclusion also suggests that if Mordecai acted in foolish pride when he refused to honor Haman, God seemed to have used Mordecai's weakness for the good. For the Bible tells me that in the month between issuing the decree to kill the Jews and the time that Mordecai and Esther were able to reverse it, that "in every providence to which the edict and order of the King came, there was great mourning among the Jews with fasting, weeping and wailing, many lay in sackcloth and ashes" (Esther 4:3). The danger led Jews everywhere to turn to God wholeheartedly! This is a perspective that each of us needs to gain. Even the disasters that may strike us are intended for our good. God is in control, and he is able to make holy our tragedies.

Esther teaches us a lesson about God's providential care. The events from which our lives and the history of nations are woven are not subject to change. They rest in the hands of a God who cares for us; a God who sometimes permits pain but is well able to transform pain into joy as we rely fully upon him.

Ecclesiastes 12:13–14 says, "Let us hear the conclusion of the whole matter: Fear God, and keep his commandments. For this is the whole duty of man. For God shall bring every work into judgment, with every secret thing, whether it be good, or whether it be evil."

The Apostle Jude's epistle concludes with a doxology: "Now unto him that is able to keep you from falling, and to present you faultless before the presence of his glory with exceeding joy, to the only wise God our Saviour, be glory and majesty, dominion and power, both now and ever. Amen" (Jude 1:24–25).

In 1 Thessalonians 5:25–28, Apostle Paul concludes, "Brethren pray for us. Greet all the brethren with a holy kiss. I charge you by the Lord that this epistle be read unto all holy brethren. The grace of our Lord Jesus Christ be with you. Amen."

There is probably no greater need in the Christian church today than its membership be made acquainted with the fundamental facts and doctrine of the Christian faith. This thesis illustrates biblical and theological teaching principles of the Bible. I hope that those who read this thesis will discover a revelation of concealed truth.

Revelation is an act of God when he communicates to the mind of man truths not known before. Inspiration is like revelation in that it is a superhuman influence upon the particular person selected to be the origin of the divine mind. It is the operation of the Holy Spirit upon the human mind for the purpose of conveying religious truth to mankind. The purpose of it is not to implant holiness but information. Inspiration is intellectual while revelation is spiritual.

The *illumination* is the understanding of truth. It is the divine quickening upon the human mind enabling it to understand truth already revealed. By truth, I mean the Holy Scriptures. My point of view is "What mind can conceive, men, women, boys, and girls can achieve—no matter what the challenge is." In Philippians 4:13, Paul stated, "I can do all things through Christ which strengthens me." My response to the Bible verse is "Oh yes, I can!"

BIBLIOGRAPHY

Boyce, E. H. *Between Now and Eternity: Eschatological Sermons.* New York: Manhattan Bible Institute, 1977.

Denney, J. *Jesus and Gospel and the Work of Jesus.* Gordon Printing Company.

Evans, W. *The Great Doctrines of the Bible.* Chicago: Moody Press, 1967.

Funk & Wagnalls. New Encyclopedia. New York: Funk & Wagnalls Publishing Co., Inc., 1946–69.

Gaverluk, E. *The Rapture Before the Russian Invasion.* Woodland, Oregon: WPT Publishing, 1988.

Hartill, J. E. *Hermeneutics.* Grand Rapids, Michigan: Zondervan Publishing House, 1970.

Henry, M. *Matthew Henry Commentary.* Grand Rapids, Michigan: Zondervan Publishing House, 1970.

King James. Analytical Bible: King James Version. Chicago: John A. Dickson Publishing Co., 1988.

Knapp, G. *Studies in Christian Doctrine.*

New Compact Webster's Dictionary. Grand Rapids, MI: Zondervan Publishing House, 1976.

Orr, J. *The Problem of the Old Testament: The Christian View of God and the World.* Kresel Publishing.

Patton, F. L. *Christian Doctrine: The Problems of the Old Testament.*

Richards, L. D. *Victor Books a Division of the Scriptures Publication: Theology in Christian Education.* Zondervan Publishing.

Schofield, C. I. The New Schofield Reference Bible: Holy Bible. New York: Oxford University Press, 1967.

Strong, A. H. *Systematic Theology.* Judson Press Publishing.

Torrey, R. A. *What the Bible Teaches: The New Topical Text Book.* Fleming H. Revell Publishing.
Ungers, M. F. *Ungers Bible Handbook.* Chicago: Moody Press, 1967.
Wood, N. *The Person and Work of Christ: The Secret of the Universe.* W.M.B. Eliman Publishing, 1955.

The late Rev. Dr. Ethel L. Williams was a longtime Christian, pastor, teacher, and missionary. She founded and pastored Mt. Calvary United Holy Church of Florence, South Carolina and Paterson, New Jersey, and Mt. Calvary Holy Church Mission of Kinston, North Carolina. A diligent and faithful servant of God, Dr. Williams helped better the lives of children and adults in her inner-city communities. Her endeavors introduced many to living a Christian life.